SPECTRUM WRITING

CONTENTS

Project Editor: Sandra Kelley
Text: Written by Craig Pearson
    Design and Production by A Good Thing, Inc.
    Illustrated by Karen Pietrobono, Kris Boyd, Doug Cushman,
        Sally Springer

Things To Remember About Writing

WRITING

- State the main idea of a paragraph in a topic sentence, and be sure all the sentences in the paragraph fit the topic.
- Use sequence words like *later* and *finally* to show the order of events and to link paragraphs in a report.
- Use comparison and contrast to make objects and events clearer.
- Use details to add strength and support to main ideas.
- Back up your opinions with facts to make them more convincing.
- Use words and phrases like *because* and *as a result* to connect ideas in cause and effect writing.
- Know your purpose before you begin to write.
- Decide on your point of view and choose the writing form that best expresses your viewpoint.

REVISING

- Use strong, exact words to improve your sentences.
- Make short, choppy sentences into longer, smoother sentences.
- Use subordinate conjunctions and relative pronouns to combine sentences.
- Correct any misplaced or dangling modifiers.

PROOFREADING

Check to see that you have
- used capitalization and punctuation correctly
- spelled all words correctly
- used the correct forms of verbs
- written quotations correctly

McGraw-Hill Children's Publishing

Copyright © 1997 McGraw-Hill Children's Publishing

Send all inquiries to:
McGraw-Hill Children's Publishing
8787 Orion Place
Columbus, OH 43240-4027

ISBN 1-57768-146-0

5 6 7 8 9 10 POH 05 04 03 02 01 00

unit 1
Writing Main Ideas

Things to Remember About Using Main Ideas in Your Writing

The **main idea** of a paragraph is what the whole paragraph is about.

Writing Tips

- State the main idea of a paragraph in a topic sentence.
- Use details in the paragraph to explain the main idea.
- Place your topic sentence first or last in the paragraph.
- Make all the sentences in the paragraph fit the topic.
- Use a topic sentence in each paragraph of an essay.

Revising Tips

- Replace vague nouns and pronouns with specific nouns and clear pronouns.

Proofreading Tips

Check to see that you have
- used capitalization and punctuation correctly
- spelled all words correctly
- used the correct forms of verbs and other words

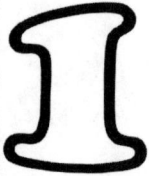

1 Stating the main idea

Read the following news story that appeared in yesterday's *Daily Trumpet*.

> George MacDonald, the ninety-two-year-old recluse who died last week, left more than $500,000 in cash to his four cats. He also left them a coin collection valued at $10,000. In addition, he willed that his twelve-room house on Elm Street would become a home for lost cats. Mr. MacDonald stated in his will that the inheritance was an expression of his gratitude for the faithful friendship of his pets Parsley, Sage, Rosemary, and Thyme.

The **main idea** of a paragraph is what the paragraph is about. It summarizes the whole paragraph. Usually, **details** in the paragraph help explain the main idea.

A. The main idea of a newspaper article is often stated in a headline. Underline the best headline for the article above.

1. **Pets Get Coin Collection**
2. **Recluse Leaves Fortune to Cats**
3. **George MacDonald Dies at Ninety-two**

B. Now list three details from the article that help explain the main idea.

_____

_____

_____

Sometimes the main idea of a paragraph is stated in a sentence. This sentence is called the **topic sentence.** The other sentences in the paragraph give details that explain the main idea.

C. Read the additional information about George MacDonald below.

During the last fifteen years, he seldom left his house.
He always kept the window shades completely closed.
One neighbor, Olga Perretti, claims she saw him only once, when he returned her son's lost cocker spaniel.
Neighbors describe MacDonald as an odd, shy man.

Decide which sentence above would make a good topic sentence for a new paragraph. Then write the paragraph below, making the topic sentence the first sentence. Complete the rest of the paragraph with the other three sentences above—the details.

_____

_____

_____

_____

_____

_____

Choose two of the headlines below. On a separate sheet of paper, write a paragraph for each headline. The headline will give the main idea, so you will need to fill in the details that explain the main idea.

Fire Destroys Empty Building
Noah Predicts Twenty More Days of Rain

New Drug Reverses Aging Process
Sixth-grade Soccer Team Triumphs

The main idea of a paragraph is what the whole paragraph is about. It is sometimes stated in one sentence, the topic sentence. The other sentences in the paragraph give details to explain the main idea.

---

2 Writing topic sentences

The topic sentence often comes first in a paragraph. However, it can appear elsewhere in the paragraph, depending on what you want to say or how you want to say it.

A. Read each paragraph below. Underline the topic sentence.

1. The Purple Knights' game against Middletown Friday was marred by six fumbles. Blockers went in wrong directions. Passes were thrown to receivers who weren't there. The players hadn't learned their plays. It's obvious from last Friday's performance that the Purple Knights need more practice to be a winning team.

2. The modern city is hard on the ears. Traffic roars constantly. Horns and sirens shake the air. Construction machines rumble underground and overhead. Even the air above is sometimes split by roaring jets streaking past.

Notice that in one paragraph the sentence that states the general idea—the topic sentence—comes first. The paragraph continues with the specifics—the detail sentences. The other paragraph starts with the specific details and builds to the topic sentence. You can choose either style, depending on whether you want to clarify the main idea by placing it first, or build up to it. Placing the main idea at or near the end of a paragraph is often done in both persuasive and mystery writing.

B. Rewrite the paragraph below. Build the suspense by placing the topic sentence at the end. Add or rearrange details if you wish.

Did my sister give me a scare last night! I thought I was alone in the house. Suddenly I heard a strange thumping noise. Then I saw weird lights moving around the basement. Nervously I asked who was there. "I'm fixing up the basement for my Halloween party," my sister called out.

_____

_____

_____

_____

C. Write a persuasive paragraph on one of the topics below. Decide whether your paragraph will work best with the topic sentence at the beginning or the end. Write at least three detail sentences. Underline your topic sentence.

why everyone should vote   why you should lend me ten dollars

_____

_____

_____

_____

Choose one of the topic sentences below. On a separate sheet of paper, write a paragraph of at least four sentences about the topic. Rearrange your paragraph by putting the topic sentence in two different positions. Put a star above the paragraph that you think works best.

I hate Mondays. ———— is a great hobby. Elephants make good pets.

The topic sentence often comes first in a paragraph, but it may also come at or near the end.

3 Keeping to the topic

A. Here is a newspaper with two front-page stories. The headlines tell you what the main ideas of the two stories are. But the printer has gotten some sentences switched from story to story. Underline the sentences that have slipped into the wrong story.

The Daily Blurt

★★★★

Cherry Trees Bloom Early

Big pink blossoms can be seen in City Park this week. The park's famous grove of cherry trees has burst into bloom three weeks earlier than usual. The group includes Tara Tiddle, guitar and vocals; Fred Frett, bass and vocals; and Archie Armwagg, drums. Mrs. Rooty said that the last time the trees bloomed this early was in 1957. The trees are expected to bear fruit in about six weeks. They will sing "Numb Noise," "I Love Miss Mess," and other songs that they made famous with their recordings.

FAMOUS SINGERS VISIT CITY

A crowd of screaming fans was on hand at City Airport this morning. They were there to welcome the Angleworms, the famous pop music group that will play Sunday at City Stadium. "Oohs" and "ahs" are heard each day from nature lovers who visit the park. This year's mild winter and heavy spring rains have caused the early blooms, according to Park Superintendent Ruth Rooty. Their Sunday afternoon concert at the stadium will begin at 2 P.M.

If sentences in a news story don't fit under the headlines, newspaper readers can become confused. Similarly, if sentences in your paragraph don't fit the topic, your readers can become confused.

B. Read the paragraph below. Underline the topic sentence. Cross out any sentences that don't fit the topic. Then, on the line provided, add your own sentence about the topic.

You need a map to find your way around Arnold's room. First, you have to step over a pile of magazines right by the door. You may not be able to see the bed since it's usually covered with games and toys. Arnold has a great game called "Stop the Spy." Most of his clothes are piled outside of his closet because the closet is filled with his collections of rocks, coins, bugs, and stamps. Arnold sure has a neat-looking green jacket.

_____

C. Complete the paragraph below. Add three detail sentences that fit the topic.

The gym was alive with color and noise the night of the class dance.

_____

_____

_____

_____

_____

Write On   Write two short news stories about something that happened this week in your school, your home, or your town or neighborhood. Write a headline for each, and be sure each sentence fits under the headline.

_____
All the sentences in a paragraph should fit the topic.

lesson 4 Writing a personal essay

An **essay** is a piece of writing that expresses a point of view about a topic. Read the two short essays below.

    My favorite time of day is early morning. I really like it then. I love to get up early and enjoy that good time of day.

    My favorite time of day is early morning. It's a quiet time, in which I can plan my day and even daydream, just thinking about whatever pops into my head. The air seems fresher somehow as I watch the sun spread new light across the sky.

A. Look back at the two essays as you complete the activities below.

1. Underline the topic sentence in each of the above essays.
2. Which essay supports its topic sentence with reasons and examples?

    _____

3. List two details from that essay.

    _____

    _____

An essay should give reasons and examples to support its point of view.

B. Which topic below do you have strong feelings about? Put an X on the line next to it.

_____ big breakfasts   _____ running   _____ tests

_____ cigarette smoking   _____ homework   _____ diets

_____ football   _____ TV   _____ politics

C. How do you feel about the topic you chose for part **B**? Do you like it, think it's bad for people, a waste of time, worth pursuing? Write a topic sentence in which you state your feelings about the topic you chose.

_____

_____

D. Now make a short outline by listing the reasons why you like or dislike your topic. Try to list at least three reasons next to the numerals below. Add others if you wish.

1. _____

_____

2. _____

_____

3. _____

_____

_____

An essay may have only one paragraph, like those at the beginning of this lesson. Longer essays have several paragraphs. In such essays, each reason or detail may serve as the topic sentence of a paragraph. Transitional words, such as _the second reason_ or _on the other hand_, often serve as a bridge to the new paragraph. For example, a second paragraph might be added to the essay on a favorite time of day beginning:

On the other hand, I dislike nighttime.

Write On On a separate sheet, write an essay of three or four paragraphs. You may wish to use the topic sentence and details you listed in parts **C** and **D**, or you may wish to broaden your topic sentence and add more details.

An essay expresses a point of view about a topic. Essays may have one paragraph or several paragraphs. Each paragraph should have a topic sentence.

---

lesson

5 **Writing a report**

An essay often expresses a personal point of view. But a **report** is based on facts. Here is one way to organize a report.

1. State the question.
2. Give the information or data.
3. Draw your conclusions.

A. Here is the report of a science experiment. Read it carefully, and then answer the questions below.

I wanted to find out if black cloth absorbs more light than white cloth. So, on a sunny day, I wrapped one ice cube in a white handkerchief and another ice cube in a black handkerchief. I put both ice cubes in the sunlight on a windowsill.

When I checked the ice cubes ten minutes later, I noticed that the ice cube in the black handkerchief had entirely melted. The ice cube in the white handkerchief was almost, but not quite, melted.

I concluded from this that the ice cube in the black handkerchief had been warmer because the black handkerchief absorbed the sunlight more than the white handkerchief. I also concluded that black or dark clothing is probably warmer in sunlight than lighter clothing.

1. What is the question asked in this experiment?

   _____

2. What were the data of this experiment?

   _____

   _____

3. What were the conclusions?

   _____

   _____

   _____

You can obtain data by performing an experiment, by taking a survey of your friends, or by checking facts in a book.

B. Choose one of the following topics to report on. Think of a question that you can answer about the topic. Then, on the lines below, fill in as much of the information as you can.

Growing Plants   TV Programming
Air Pollution   Hobbies

1. Question: _____

_____

2. Data (list what you know or how you will obtain data): _____

_____

_____

_____

3. Conclusion: _____

_____

_____

Write On

If you haven't done so, collect the rest of your data and fill in your conclusion. Then, on a separate sheet of paper, write a report of at least three paragraphs on your topic.

A report is based on facts. Many reports include a question to be answered; information or data from experiments, books, or surveys; and a conclusion.

Revising

6 Choosing nouns and pronouns

When you **revise** something you've written, you read it over, changing words to make them more specific and combining sentences to make them smoother. In Lesson 6 of every unit, we'll look at one aspect of revising. First, let's look at nouns and pronouns.

You might not pay much attention if someone told you, "My animal buried the thing." But suppose that person said, "My puppy buried your wallet." That sentence would grab your attention, wouldn't it?

Remember that when you are writing, you are sending messages and trying to grab your readers' attention. One way to write effective and clear messages is to use **specific nouns.**

A. Next to each general noun below, write three more specific nouns.

1. Animal: _____

2. Person: _____

3. Food: _____

4. Clothing: _____

5. Building: _____

B. Here's another vague message.

Quentin drank the liquid.

Quentin could be drinking hot cocoa, rat poison, or any other "subcategory" of liquid. You can create an interesting situation by substituting a specific noun for the general category word *liquid*. Improve the sentence by substituting a specific noun for *liquid*. Then add two or three sentences that tell more about what happened.

_____

_____

_____

_____

_____

Pronouns also can be too general. Each pronoun you use should clearly refer to a noun. In the sentence "Magda gave Alice her book," the girl *her* refers to is unclear. The revision "Magda gave Alice's book back" is clearer.

C. Fix each pronoun problem below by revising the sentences.
   1. There was a loud gunshot. Then he rushed downstairs and out the door. (He could be any male—human, cat, dog, monkey, Martian, and so on.)

   _____

   _____

   2. Great-aunt Clementine went everywhere with her poodle Suzette. She always wore pink ribbons around her ears. (Who did? Great-aunt Clementine?)

   _____

   _____

   3. I hung my wig out on the roof to dry. It blew off during the storm last night. (What blew off?)

   _____

   _____

Write On   Look over the "Write On" papers you have written for this unit. Check for vague nouns and sloppy pronouns. Choose a paper that could be clearer and revise it.

Use specific nouns and clear pronouns when you write.

Proofreading

Checking your writing

suppose we never used punctuation marks or capital letters in writing do you think sentences and paragraphs would be hard to read can you see why puntuation and capitalization are helpful to readers

A. The paragraph above has no capital letters or punctuation marks. Rewrite it correctly on the lines below.

_____

_____

_____

_____

After you have finished writing and revising your work, it is a good idea to proofread it to check on your capitalization, punctuation, spelling, and word usage. You can correct any errors on your paper by making changes like those below.

Mrs. gimble backed slow into the parking place then she heard a scraping noise. "Oh! she sighs. "What'll I do now?"

B. Proofread and correct the paragraph below. Follow the sample above. Watch out for capitalization, punctuation, spelling, and word usage.

The peeple had been on the island for weeks since the shipwreck suddenly they seen a plane flying overhead. They waves and shouted, but the plan keeped going?

C. On the lines below, write a paragraph telling what might happen next to the people on the island. Proofread your writing to be sure it's correct.

_____

_____

_____

_____

_____

_____

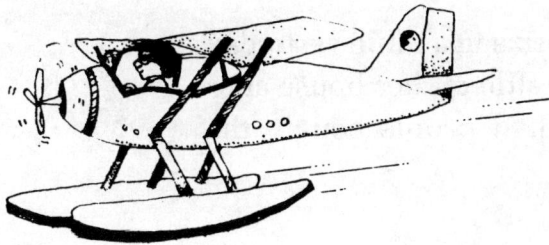

As you proofread your writing, check to see:

- that capitalization and punctuation are used correctly
- that your words are spelled correctly
- that you have used the correct forms of words

1. Read the following paragraph from a news story. Then underline the best headline for it.

    Mrs. Mary Dowd gave away her home as first prize in a raffle yesterday in Drury, Illinois. Mrs. Dowd said she decided to raffle off her house after trying unsuccessfully to sell her home. Six hundred people bought the $100 raffle tickets, bringing in $60,000.

    a. Housing Industry Slumps
    b. Raffles Become Popular Fund-Raisers
    c. A House Raffle in Illinois

2. Read this paragraph from a report. Then underline the purpose of the paragraph in the report.

    I wanted to study animal life in my backyard. To do this, I observed my backyard for two months. I tried to watch it at different times of day, especially at dawn and at sunset.

    This paragraph
    a. states the question asked in the experiment.
    b. gives the data of the experiment.
    c. states the conclusions.

3. Read the following paragraph. Then write a topic sentence for it.

    Some children played ice hockey on the lake. Others practiced spins and turns on their figure skates. Smaller children skated awkwardly on double-bladed skates, while dogs simply skidded across the ice, barking excitedly.

    Topic sentence: _____

4. Write a humorous one-paragraph personal essay on the following topic:
    Why My Worst Habit Is Really Lovable

unit 2
Writing in Sequence

Things to Remember About Writing in Sequence

Sequence tells the order of events.

Writing Tips

- Use sequence words and phrases like *now*, *later*, *finally*, and *at last* to clearly show the order of events.
- Use words like *above*, *below*, and *on the right* to tell where things are.
- Use words like *first*, *next*, and *last* when you write directions.
- Use an outline to organize your information and the sequence of your paragraphs.
- Use sequence words to link paragraphs in a report.
- End your report with a summary statement or paragraph.

Revising Tips

- Use powerful, active verbs to strengthen your sentences.
- Use strong verbs only when they are appropriate.

Proofreading Tips

Check to see that you have

- begun every important word of a proper noun with a capital letter

Writing a narrative in sequence

A, B, C, D, . . . What comes next? The answer is easy, because each item is a part of a well-known **sequence.**

Now look at the picture below. What will happen next?

Most likely, the woman will eat her dinner. But if the woman is a character in your story, you can make anything happen. Since your readers don't know what to expect, you must be especially careful to order phrases and sentences so that the readers know, as clearly as *A-B-C*, what happens step by step.

A. Here are some events that might go into a story about the woman in the picture above. Number them in an order that makes sense.

_____ Suddenly there was a knock on the door.

_____ Then Cornelius Van Loony, Mrs. Van Loony's long-lost husband, staggered into the room.

_____ Mrs. Van Loony was just about to start eating her lobster dinner.

_____ "I didn't die eight years ago—I was stranded on a desert island," he gasped.

_____ As the butler started toward the door, it opened.

_____ After he said this, he collapsed at the foot of the table.

Did any words help you order the sentences? Words like _then_ and _after_ can help make the sequence of events clear. Some other **sequence words and phrases** are _now_, _later_, _finally_, and _at last_.

B. Now write your own story. On the lines below, finish the story any way you wish. Just be sure that the sequence of events is clear.

Mrs. Van Loony was just about to start eating her lobster dinner, when

suddenly _____

_____

_____

_____

_____

_____

_____

_____

Write On
Did you ever look at a clean, unused pair of sneakers in a shoe store and wonder what its life is going to be like? If you haven't, think about the excitement, the wear and tear, the travel. Write a short "biography" of a pair of sneakers (perhaps your own). Remember to write so that the sequence of events is clear.

Events in a story occur in a certain sequence. Sequence words like <u>then</u>, <u>now</u>, <u>later</u>, <u>finally</u>, and <u>at last</u> help make the order clear.

lesson

2 Writing an explanation in sequence

Who stole the priceless diamond?

The best way to give an **explanation** of how things happen is to write a clear sequence of events.

A. Can you reconstruct the crime pictured above? Complete the sentences below by writing an explanation of the theft as it probably happened.

The first thing the thief did was _____

_____

Next, he _____

_____

_____

Finally, _____

_____

_____

Besides using time order in an explanation, you may need to tell where things are in relation to each other. Words and phrases like *near, far, above, below, on the right,* and *on the left* make some explanations easier to understand.

B. The picture shows an invention called the water alarm. It is guaranteed to wake you up. On the lines below, explain how the invention works. In your explanation, make the time sequence clear and explain where things are in relation to each other.

_____

_____

_____

_____

_____

Write On

Suppose that your best friend lives directly above you in an apartment building. Your bedroom windows face the same way. Can you invent a private communication system so that you can pass notes and other things from one window to the other? Perhaps you will use a clothesline, or even a helium-filled balloon. On another sheet of paper, explain clearly how your invention works. Draw a picture if you wish.

A clear explanation should be written in sequence. Some explanations also use words like <u>above</u>, <u>below</u>, and <u>on the right</u> to tell where things are.

3 Writing "how to" directions in sequence

A clear sequence is especially important when you write **directions.** Sequence words like *first, next,* and *last* can be helpful. Sometimes directions are written step by step, with each step numbered.

A. Below are directions for a simple card trick—that is, it would be a simple trick if the directions were written in the proper order. Read over the directions. Then number the steps in the correct order.

———— Shuffle the cards.

———— Ask your victim to pick a card from the deck and look at it without showing it to you.

———— Use a deck of cards with a picture on the back.

———— Make sure all the pictures are facing you before you start the trick.

———— When the victim returns the card, make sure that the picture on the card goes in facing away from you. (It will be the only card facing the opposite direction.)

———— Look for the card. To be convincing, study a few cards, trying to make up your mind—but you are really looking for the one card with the picture facing the other way.

———— Important: Be sure when you shuffle that you keep the pictures facing the same way or you'll never be able to find the card.

B. Look at the map. Suppose an out-of-town friend is coming to visit. He must call first at the Jones Company. Then he wants to drive to your house. On the lines below, write clear directions for him. Use street names, stoplights, and names of buildings to make your directions clear. Watch out for one-way streets.

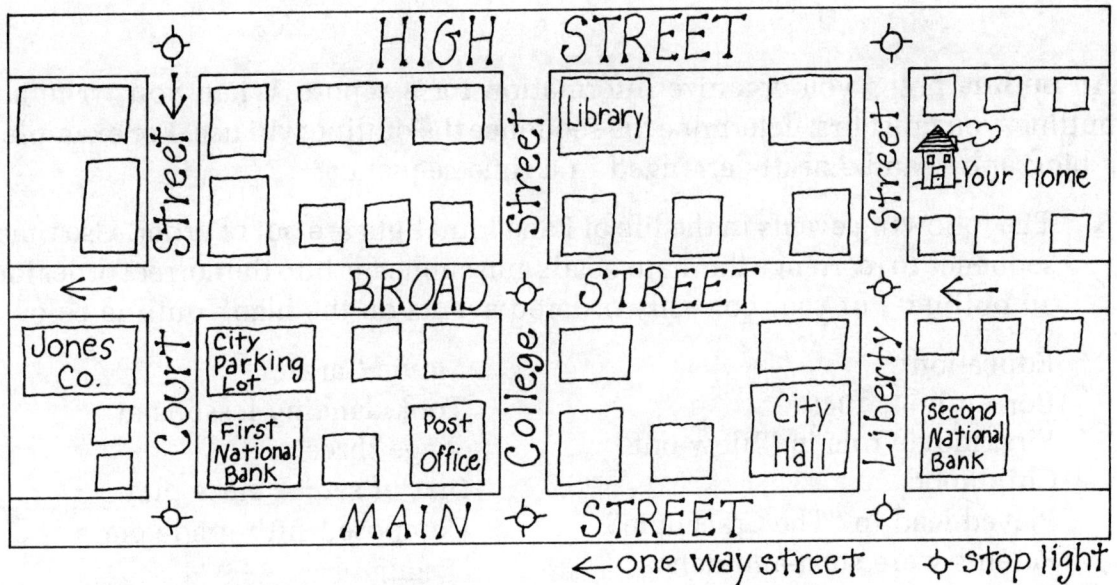

_____

_____

_____

_____

_____

_____

Write On

Think of a simple task that you can do well. Then, on a separate sheet of paper, write directions that will help someone else do the same task for the first time. Choose your own subject or one of these:

how to print a capital *B*
how to hammer a nail into a board
how to thread a needle

how to add 16 and 7
how to make cinnamon toast
how to hold a baseball bat

A clear, step-by-step sequence is important when you write directions.

4 Writing an outline in sequence

An **outline** helps you organize information for a report. When you write an outline, you must first determine the sequence the outline will use. For example, a biography can be neatly arranged in a time sequence.

A. The following events in the life of Lana Limelight are out of order. Use time sequence to rearrange the main heads and subheads into the correct order for an outline. Put your correctly ordered events on the blank outline below.

Education
Born July 4, 1940
First movie role in "Blow-out"
Childhood
Played lead in "The Crabapple"
Parents were song-and-dance
  team

Movie Career
Took dancing lessons at
  age three
Star of senior class play
Composed fifth-grade class
  song
Discovered in soda shop

I. _____

    A. _____

    B. _____

    C. _____

II. _____

    A. _____

    B. _____

III. _____

    A. _____

    B. _____

    C. _____

B. Other kinds of outlines can be organized in different ways. Suppose you are writing a report about the mythical country Disturbia. You want to describe briefly these four areas: Government, Geography, Major Cities, and Economy. Decide which order you will arrange the topics in, and fill in the headings on the blank outline below part **C.**

C. Once the main heads are arranged in a workable sequence, you can fill in the subheads below them. Fill in the following subheads under the correct main heads on the blank outline below.

Coastline	Winkle (county seat)	Cheeseburg
Zinc mining	Great Plains	Kokola Jungle
Grunt (county seat)	Calabash Mountain	Umbrella manufacturing
County councils	Blithney (capital)	Royal advisors
Congress	King and Queen	Leading vacation land
	Growing radishes	

I. _____   III. _____

   A. _____   A. _____

   B. _____   B. _____

   C. _____   C. _____

   D. _____   D. _____

II. _____   IV. _____

   A. _____   A. _____

   B. _____   B. _____

   C. _____   C. _____

   D. _____   D. _____

Write On

Choose a topic of special interest to you: your life, your city or state, your school, and so on. Decide on at least three main headings to use in writing about the topic. Then decide which sequence of headings works best. Write them down (on a separate sheet of paper). Fill in at least two subheadings under each by adding supporting facts and ideas to your outline.

An outline uses a sequence to help you organize ideas for a report.

---

5 Writing a report from an outline

Outlines are used to organize information for a **report.** Be sure your report follows the order of your outline, unless you make a decision to reorganize it. Don't leave out any subheadings, and don't write facts in one paragraph that belong in a different section.

A. Here are part of the outline of Disturbia and a paragraph based on it. Read them, and answer the questions below.

IV. Government
  A. County councils
  B. Congress
  C. Royal advisors
  D. King and Queen

  The national government of Disturbia is ruled by King Anton the Angry and Queen Bella Gerint. They, in turn, are counseled by royal advisors Sir Worry Wart and U.N. Settle. They all live in Blithney, the lovely capital city, nestled at the foot of Calabash Mountain. As far as local government goes, there are county councils whose members are elected by the voters every six weeks.

1. Does this paragraph follow the outline? How is it different?

_____

2. Which subheading was left out?

_____

3. Which sentence fits under a different part of the outline?

_____

B. Here is another part of the outline of Disturbia.

III. Major Cities
  A. Blithney (capital)
  B. Grunt (county seat)
  C. Winkle (county seat)
  D. Cheeseburg

On the lines below, write a paragraph that follows the outline. Make up some facts about each city. Be sure to discuss them in the right order.

_____

_____

_____

_____

_____

_____

C. **Sequence words and phrases** often help to link together paragraphs or parts of reports. Can you add some sequence words to the list below?

after   _____   _____

as soon as   _____   _____

finally   _____   _____

D. A report often ends with a **summary statement or paragraph.** Which statement below do you think is the better summary for the report on Disturbia? Put a check mark on the line before it.

_____ That is all I can think of to say about Disturbia.

_____ Thus, we can see that Disturbia is a country with many problems, but with the resources and leadership to find the right solutions.

Write On On separate paper, write a report based on the outline you wrote for Lesson 4. Keep in mind what you've practiced in this lesson. Make your report three or more paragraphs long.

When you write a report, follow your outline. Use sequence words to link paragraphs, and end with a summary statement or paragraph.

Revising

Choosing verbs

Pay special attention to your **verbs** as you revise your writing. Verbs pack power into a sentence.

When you can, try to replace forms of *be* with a more powerful verb. Look at the revisions below.

Weak: Chico was opposed to the plan.
More Powerful: Chico disagreed with the plan.
Weak: Kathy was happy.
More Powerful: Kathy grinned.

A. Revise each sentence below to make the verb more powerful.

1.   Agnes was unhappy.

_____

2.   Dad was angry with me.

_____

3.   It was a hot, sunny day.

_____

4.   I was frightened in the long, dark alley.

_____

Use the **active voice** rather than the **passive voice** as much as possible. Passive verbs are made up of *be* plus the verb form used with *has (was done)*. Active-voice verbs are more powerful. Look at the revision below.

Passive: The hooting of an owl was heard.
Active: An owl hooted.

B. Revise each sentence below to change the verb to the active voice.

1.   The cake was baked by Jake.

_____

2. A decree was issued by the queen.

_____

3. Our dog was chased by two cats.

_____

4. A speeding car was seen on the road.

_____

Use **strong verbs** whenever possible, but don't use them when inappropriate. Look at these examples.

Weak: Gino said that he was falling over the cliff.
Strong: Gino screamed that he was falling over the cliff.

Inappropriate: Erica asserted that it was a nice day.
Better: Erica said that it was a nice day.

C. Revise any sentences below that you think need stronger verbs. Leave any that you think are OK.

1. The starving puppy ate the food.

_____

2. Jules walks to school every day.

_____

3. Marcy went into the theater twenty minutes late for rehearsal.

_____

4. The small child carried a large package.

_____

Look back over the "Write On" exercises you've written for this unit. Pay special attention to the verbs you've used. Have you used strong, active verbs wherever appropriate? Choose one "Write On" to revise on another sheet of paper.

_____

Use powerful, active verbs wherever appropriate in your writing.

Proofreading

Using capital letters correctly

You know that the first word of every sentence begins with a capital letter. You also capitalize **proper nouns**—names of particular people and places.

Look at the list of rules and examples below.

1. **Capitalize names of people and pets, people's initials and titles, and the pronoun** I.

   Mickey Mouse   O. J. Simpson   Dr. Brothers

2. **Capitalize names of days, months, and holidays.**
   Tuesday   September   Columbus Day

3. **Capitalize names of geographical places—streets, towns and cities, rivers, mountains, lakes, oceans, states, countries, continents.**

   Elm Street   Newburgh   Pacific Ocean
   Mt. Rainier   Peru   Africa

4. **Capitalize names of businesses and organizations, buildings, schools, parks, and brand names. Notice that small words like of and the are not capitalized when they are part of proper nouns.**

   Mort's Meat Market   Tower of London   Central Park
   American Red Cross   Antioch College   Smilee toothpaste

A. Rewrite only the word groups below that need capital letters.
   1. doctor, doctor althea j. gonzalez, dog, lassie

   _____

   2. rocky mountains, a large lake, missouri river

   _____

   3. a wide avenue, a small town, minneapolis, north america

   _____

   4. golden gate park, a new soft drink, elsie's knitting boutique

   _____

   5. good day, sunday, fourth of july, a winter month

   _____

B. Proofread and correct these sentences. Write in capital letters where they are needed.

1. on our vacation, last august my family and i visited the grand canyon and lake tahoe.

2. my mother voted for president carter in the last election.

3. last november p. j. reynolds visited paris, france.

4. on cold winter mornings, my mother gives me a hot bowl of lumper's oatmeal—and i hate it.

5. my father works for the smithville corporation, one of the biggest companies in north america.

6. sammy's pizza parlor, which is located on sunnyside boulevard, has the best pizza in town.

7. my sister stephanie is studying at harvard university to become a lawyer.

8. my dog rover was a gift from uncle al last christmas.

9. when i had pneumonia last february, dr. small made me take liver's cough syrup, which was the worst medicine i had ever tasted.

10. terry bradshaw, the quarterback for the pittsburgh steelers, played in the super bowl last year.

Begin every important word of a proper noun with a capital letter. Proper nouns name particular people, places, and things.

Post-Test

1. The outline below is for a report on the Aztec Indians. Write the parts of the outline in the correct order.

   Arts   Three Ruling Classes
   Religious Beliefs   Aztec Government
   Aztec Culture   Wars with Neighboring Tribes

   I. _____   II. _____

      A. _____   A. _____

      B. _____   B. _____

2. Below is a set of directions on how to bowl. Number the steps in the correct sequence.

   _____ Hold the ball up to your chest and stand on the starting line.

   _____ Pick up the ball by placing your first three fingers in the finger-holes.

   _____ Find a ball that is as heavy as you can comfortably carry.

   _____ Release the ball on the third step.

   _____ Take three steps forward as you swing the ball.

3. Suppose you wanted to tame a wild animal, like a dolphin, a whale, or a baby lion. Explain how you would do it in a short paragraph. Use sequence words to describe how your friendship grows.

4. Revise these sentences by using a verb in the active voice or by using a stronger verb.
   a. A picture of the UFO was taken by Bert.

   _____

   b. The sun was bright on the ocean waves.

   _____

   c. The audience was amazed by the magician.

   _____

unit 3
Writing Comparisons

Things to Remember About
Writing Comparisons

Comparisons show likenesses. **Contrasts** show differences.

Writing Tips
- Use comparison and contrast to make objects and events clearer.
- Use similes and metaphors to make your writing more colorful. Remember that a simile contains *like* or *as*. A metaphor says one thing is another thing.
- Avoid using tired similes and mixed metaphors.
- Make your character descriptions sharper by comparing and contrasting the characters.

Revising Tips
- Use specific adjectives to make your descriptions clearer.

Proofreading Tips Check to see that you have
- used commas correctly to separate words, word groups, and clauses

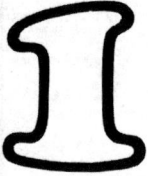

1 Writing about likenesses and differences

A. Can you answer the riddles below? Try them before you check the answers on page 126.

1. How is a fiction book like a tall building?

   _____

2. What's the difference between a jeweler and a prison guard?

   _____

3. Why is baseball like cake?

   _____

4. What's the difference between a thief and a seat belt?

   _____

5. When is candy like a government building?

   _____

Many riddles and jokes are based on **comparisons,** which show likenesses, and **contrasts,** which show differences. Serious writers also compare and contrast to make objects and events clearer.

B. Some things which seem very different may turn out—when you think about them—to be alike in some ways. Choose two of the pairs below and explain how they are alike.

   a sunset and a butterfly   a piece of clay and a pen
   a garden and a kitchen   a quilt and a fireplace

1. _____

   _____

2. _____

   _____

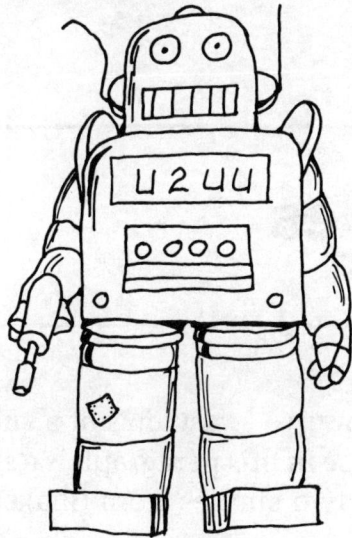

C. The two robots above are alike or similar in many ways and different in other ways. First, make a list of their similarities. Then use the two columns to list their differences.

Similarities

_____

_____

_____

Differences

_____   _____

_____   _____

_____   _____

_____

You can write a comparison paragraph by discussing similarities first, and then tell about differences.

Write On

Choose one pair below. On a separate sheet of paper, make a list of similarities and differences. Then write a comparison paragraph.

a school bus and a city bus   a TV show and a movie
a rainstorm and a snowstorm   breakfast and dinner

Writers compare by showing likenesses and contrast by showing differences. Comparison and contrast can help to make objects and events clearer.

2 Writing similes

A **simile** is like a double mirror. The writer can give two views of a subject by comparing it to something else. The first sentence in this paragraph is a simile. A simile compares by using *like* or *as*. Here are two similes from Shakespeare.

Study is like the heaven's glorious sun.
I'll say she looks as clear as morning roses washed with dew.

A. Similes can give sentences more life and meaning. Complete the simile in the second version of each sentence below.

1. Ed's hands were cold.
   Ed's hands felt as cold as _____.
2. Ellen was very busy.
   Ellen was as busy as _____.
3. Millie was pretty.
   Millie was as pretty as _____.
4. Eric never stopped working.
   Eric worked like _____.
5. Sarah felt out of place.
   Sarah felt like _____.
6. Joe was very hungry.
   Joe was as hungry as _____.

Did you use similes such as *cold as ice, busy as a bee,* and *pretty as a picture?* These similes were once new and fresh. They've been used so often, however, that they are no longer likely to catch the reader's attention. They are **clichés.** A tired simile can come alive when you change the comparison. "Busy as a bee" might become "busy as a snowplow in a blizzard."

B. Nine more clichés are listed below. On the lines that follow, write new similes to replace five of the clichés.

cool as a cucumber	fat as a pig	fresh as a daisy
dead as a doornail	flat as a pancake	gentle as a lamb
eyes like stars	strong as an ox	sleep like a log

1. _____.

2. _____

3. _____

4. _____

5. _____

Write On

Look at the picture of the beach. How does it make you feel? Write a paragraph describing the scene—the beach, the sea, and your feelings about any or all of them. Use at least four similes in your paragraph.

A simile compares two things by using like or as. Fresh similes give life to writing.

lesson

3 Writing metaphors

A **metaphor** is a mirror in which two images practically blend. Instead of saying that one thing is *like* another, in a metaphor the writer says that one thing *is* another. The first sentence of this paragraph is a metaphor. Here are two of Shakespeare's many metaphors:

The world's mine oyster, which I with sword will open.
The web of our life is of a mingled yarn, good and ill together.

A. List the two things being compared in each metaphor above.

_____

_____

A metaphor can be extended into a paragraph. Here is part of an extended metaphor.

School is a supermarket in which the wise shopper must move with care. Some shoppers dash through the aisles, missing good values, stopping only at the candy and bakery sections. Other shoppers buy more sensibly, choosing many foods for a balanced diet. In the same way, wise students. . . .

B. Choose one of the metaphors below and continue it like the model above.

Life is a flower garden.
Writing is a game.
Learning is pick-and-shovel work.
Youth is a spring storm.
Friendship is a seesaw.

_____

_____

_____

_____

_____

Sometimes a writer wants a metaphor to be funny. Sometimes, though, the joke is accidental. Think about this metaphor.

Jack's imagination was an express train leaping from topic to topic.

What's wrong with that? Can a train leap? We call this a **mixed metaphor**. The writer has mixed two images—that of an express train and that of leaping—and the mixture doesn't work. The sentence might be revised to read "Jack's imagination leaped from topic to topic like a frog in a hurry" or "Jack's imagination was an express train traveling rapidly from topic to topic."

C. Here are three more mixed metaphors. Rewrite each one so that the metaphor is unmixed.

1. There was Miyoshi, a beautiful flower walking through an ocean of weeds.

    _____

    _____

2. Mike was a high-powered truck, loaded with heavy boxes yet jumping down the road.

    _____

    _____

3. The wind was a wild vacuum cleaner, pulling trees out by their roots and chewing up rooftops.

    _____

    _____

Write On

What if you were a motor vehicle. What kind would you be? Would you think of yourself as a tractor-trailer, a sports car, a stock car, a jeep, a luxury car, a pickup truck? Write a paragraph, beginning "I am a (type of vehicle) . . ." and continuing the metaphor.

_____

Metaphors compare two unlike things without using <u>like</u> or <u>as</u>. A metaphor can be extended into a whole paragraph. Careful writers avoid mixed metaphors.

Making up humorous names

What's in a name? A lot of fun, sometimes. Some writers make up metaphoric names for their characters. Names may describe characters by comparing them to objects or by including adjectives that describe the way a person looks. In *James and the Giant Peach*, for example, Aunt Sponge is fat and flabby while Aunt Spiker is tall and bony. In *Peter Pan*, Captain Hook is named for the hook that replaces his hand. Look at the pictures below to see some other humorous names for characters.

Scruffy McFilth

Poodles O'Hare

A. Try to think of a humorous name to fit each character described below.

1. a short, pudgy man with a big black mustache

_____

2. a wise-looking girl with large, round glasses

_____

3. an elderly, stooped man with a long white beard

_____

4. a thin, birdlike woman

_____

5. a huge man, tall, heavy, and muscular

_____

Sometimes names describe personality or behavior, rather than physical appearance. For example, an inventor named Gyro Gearloose is probably a little cracked, whereas Worthy Upright is a fine, upstanding citizen.

B. Try naming each person below to describe what he or she is like.

1. a clumsy man who works in a bank

   _____

2. a woman who works very hard washing, ironing, and cleaning

   _____

3. a daredevil who races cars, planes, and boats

   _____

4. a very rich girl who loves to go to parties and meet famous people

   _____

5. a detective who always tracks down the criminal

   _____

A character can be named simply for his or her occupation. In this case, a writer might choose a name that sounds like part of the job. Weather forecasters might be called Hugh Midity or Hy Winz. A service station attendant might be Phil R. Upp; a tailor, Pat Chezz.

C. Think of a sound-alike name for each character below.

1. a musician _____

2. a gardener _____

3. a comedian _____

4. a cook _____

Invent a name for a town and two characters who live there. Describe each in one paragraph—that is, write three paragraphs in all.

Names can be metaphors that describe characters in a humorous way.

41

5 Writing to compare characters

A character description will often be clearer if characters are compared and contrasted.

A. Study the two pictures below. Then write a paragraph about the two, concentrating on the ways in which they are *alike*.

_____

_____

_____

_____

_____

B. Study the four pictures on page 43. Choose two of the people as characters in a short-short story you plan to write. Make up names for both of them and write each name under the person's picture. Then, on the lines provided, write notes about your two characters to show how they are alike and how they are different.

_____   _____

_____   _____

_____   _____

_____   _____

Here is the situation for your short-short story: For the past month, a mysterious burglar has been breaking into homes throughout the community. The burglar steals school books—nothing else. Your two characters get together and try to think up ways to stop this crime wave. Write the story on a separate sheet of paper.

A character description will often be clearer if characters are compared and contrasted.

Revising

6 Choosing adjectives

Adjectives help you describe objects and characters.

    <u>taller</u> robot   <u>striped</u> shirt   <u>pudgy</u> man

    Specific, concrete adjectives give clearer descriptions than adjectives like *nice, funny,* or *awful.*

The nice woman looked funny when the awful thing happened.

A. Revise the description of the scene in the picture. In three or four sentences, describe the way each person is dressed, how each person looks and feels, and what happened. Use specific adjectives.

_____

_____

_____

_____

_____

Adjectives should be used with care. Sometimes a writer is tempted to use piles of adjectives to make up for weak nouns and verbs. Read this example.

Fritz was a bold, adventurous, wild, chance-taking player until a terrible, tragic thing happened.

Compare the sentence above to its revision below.

Fritz was a daring player. Then tragedy struck.

B. Some of the sentences below might be improved by adding adjectives. Others have too many adjectives already. Revise each sentence.

1. Tom groaned when he saw the lawn.

_____

2. Happy, smiling, and refreshed, Juanita looked up at the bright, sun-touched, billowing, soft, white clouds in the sky.

_____

3. Marisa felt sorry for the dog.

_____

4. The roaring, whistling, smoke-throwing, screeching cars came down the track.

_____

5. The old, elderly, gray-haired woman sat on a hard, stiff, uncomfortable wooden bench.

_____

Write On
Look over the "Write On" papers you have written for this unit. Check for writing that can use more specific adjectives or that is overloaded with adjectives. Choose one "Write On" that needs revision and rewrite it on another sheet of paper.

_____

Use specific adjectives to write descriptions, but do not overload your sentences with adjectives.

Proofreading

7

Using commas correctly

Commas are used to signal slight separations between written words—or pauses in speech. Follow these rules for using commas.

1. **Use commas to separate the day and the year in a date and the street, city, and state or country in an address.**

    July 3, 1979, was the date of the big game.
    It was held at a park on West Street, Allenville, Maryland.

2. **Use commas to separate items in a series.**

    The players were hot, tired, and thirsty.

3. **Use commas to separate two or more coordinate, or equal, adjectives.**

    The hot, thirsty players drank lots of water.

4. **Use commas to set off introductory words, such as <u>well</u> or <u>yes</u>, and the names of people being spoken to.**

    Yes, we won the game.
    Larry, you played well.

5. **Use commas to set off a group of words that follow a noun and give information about it. Such word groups are often called appositives.**

    Mr. Mannheim, owner of the meat market, sponsored our team.

6. **Use commas to separate compound sentences joined by conjunctions. Use a comma to separate an introductory subordinate clause from the main clause.**

    We had played well, and we were happy.
    Since we had played well, we were happy.

A. Put in commas where they are needed in the sentences below.

1. On April 5 1922 our rocket left Nome Alaska.
2. Edgar Bernier the navigator of the ship was a cautious prudent chap.
3. Yes I was surprised that we got lost in space.
4. Weren't you surprised Emily?
5. The pilot the navigator and the crew were worried.

6. When we saw Mars we all felt better.

7. It looked far-off strange and unfriendly but we were still glad to see it.

B. Proofread and correct this paragraph. Add end marks, commas, and capital letters where they are needed.

my brother loves to play practical jokes on april 1 1979 he carried around a water pistol a rubber snake and a pen filled with disappearing ink did he cause problems well he had his fun that day but he spent a lot of time with mrs shellabarger the principal

When you proofread your writing, check to see that you have used commas correctly. Follow the rules on page 46.

Post-Test

1. Write a paragraph comparing the two characters in the picture above.

2. Write two similarities and two differences between a sailboat and a cloud.

   Similarities   Differences

   _____   _____

   _____   _____

3. Write one metaphor and one simile, using the words below or your own.

   kangaroo   math problem   sandpaper
   younger brother or sister   burnt toast   quicksand

   Metaphor _____

   Simile _____

4. Put commas where they are needed in the sentences below.

   a. Laurel was born on May 23 1971.

   b. We ordered a sandwich a bowl of chili and two glasses of milk.

   c. No I haven't seen *Star Troubles* but I may see it next Saturday.

unit 4
Writing Details

Things to Remember About Writing with Details

Details are small bits of information.

Writing Tips
- Use details to add strength and support to main ideas.
- Look carefully at all the details in a picture before you decide on the main idea of a description you are writing.
- Use your five senses to gather details when writing descriptions of objects.
- Use details that make a character special when writing character descriptions.
- Use strange or unusual details when writing a mystery.

Revising Tips
- Use adverbs and adverbial phrases to tell *when*, *where*, and *how*.
- Eliminate adverbs when a strong verb can do the job by itself.

Proofreading Tips Check to see that you have
- used the plain form of present-tense verbs with *I*, *you*, and plural subjects
- used the *s* form of present-tense verbs with singular nouns and pronouns
- used the correct present-and past-tense forms of the verb *be*
- written correctly those verbs that change their spelling to make the *s* form

Writing about details in a picture

Details in a picture add texture, interest, and support. In a similar way, details in a written paragraph add strength and support to main ideas.

A. Look at the picture below. Then, on the following lines, write a main idea about it.

_____

_____

B. Look at the picture again. Note four details that support your main idea.

1. _____

2. _____

3. _____

4. _____

Writers sometimes have to look closely—some of the details in a situation may be "hidden" from view.

C. Look more closely at the right-hand side of the picture. Then note four more details that support or change your main idea.

1. _____

2. _____

3. _____

4. _____

D. Write a paragraph about the scene in the picture. Use your original or revised main idea to write a topic sentence. Then write at least four additional sentences about the details that support your topic.

_____

_____

_____

_____

_____

_____

Write On On another sheet of paper, write a main idea about your own classroom. Then look very carefully around the room. List all the details you can that make the classroom what it is. (You may be surprised to find you are really seeing some details for the first time.) These details will help you decide whether to keep or change your first main idea. Then write a paragraph about your classroom, with a topic sentence and details that support it.

Look carefully at all the details before you decide on the main idea or topic sentence of a descriptive paragraph.

2 Writing an encyclopedia entry

Each year in school you learn more and more facts. A **fact** is a type of detail. Taking care of details is a little like keeping a room clean. Details are most useful when you put them where they belong. Just as you might put shirts in one drawer and books on a shelf, so must you arrange details. One place where you'll find many facts, all arranged under topics, is an **encyclopedia.**

A. You receive a letter from the *Encyclopedia of Famous Rooms.* They have heard about your famous bedroom, and they want you to write an entry for the encyclopedia. Fill in the information requested below.

1. Address? _____

2. Where in the building is your bedroom? _____

3. Who uses this room? _____

4. How long have you used this room? _____

5. What do you like best about it? _____

6. List four or five interesting details about the contents or arrangement of

    your room. _____

    _____

    _____

    _____

Encyclopedia entries must often be short. They can include only the most important details.

B. You get this telegram from the encyclopedia editors: "Help STOP Computer made mistake STOP We got 3,000,000 entries STOP Cut your entry to 75 words STOP Tell only most important details STOP Cut rest STOP Use complete sentences STOP Eds." On the blank lines, rewrite the entry you wrote for part **A.** Be sure you write seventy-five words or less.

_____

_____

_____

_____

_____

_____

C. Choose an animal that you are interested in. You will write about that animal for the *Encyclopedia Britictactoe.* How would you organize information about the animal for an encyclopedia entry of two hundred words or less? Write an outline to show how you would organize the facts. Look back at the outline on page 25 if you need help setting yours up.

_____

_____

_____

_____

_____

_____

On a separate sheet of paper, write your encylcopedia entry. Follow the outline you made for part **C.**

Encyclopedias list facts arranged by topic. A fact is a type of detail. Sometimes, for short encyclopedia entries, only the most important details are included.

3 Describing an object with sense words

How would you describe an object to someone who has never seen it? Explorers to new worlds often find new plants and animals. They use their **senses** to learn details about the look, sound, smell, taste, and feel of these new things.

A. Pretend that you are an explorer returning to Spain from the New World. You discovered a new vegetable there—corn. The sample that you brought back was ruined, however, so you must use words to describe corn to the King and Queen. In ten minutes, you are to go before the throne to speak. To prepare your speech, use all your five senses to list details about the vegetable. Then write your ideas in sentences.

How it looks: _____

How it feels: _____

How it tastes: _____

How it smells: _____

How it sounds (when shucked or later): _____

Sentences: _____

_____

_____

_____

_____

B. On your next trip back to the New World, you tell the Native Americans about horses. (There were no horses in the New World when the first Europeans landed.) Write a paragraph about horses. Describe more than their appearance. Examine horses with as many senses as you can.

_____

_____

_____

_____

_____

_____

_____

Write On

A Martian has just knocked on your door. You decide your visitor will feel friendlier with something to eat. Choose something that's in your kitchen, like an orange or a stalk of celery. Before you can go to the kitchen, the Martian wants to know what you are getting. Since your visitor understands only written English, you will need to write a description. List sense details about the food in the same way you did for corn. Then write a descriptive paragraph about the food to make what it is clear to a Martian.

Using our five senses provides us with many details to help in writing a description of an object.

55

4 Describing a character

You had saved for months to make a special purchase. You felt great as you left the store. You could hardly wait to get home to try out your new treasure. You glanced for a minute at these two people as you stood at the bus stop.

A minute later, these two bumped into you, grabbed your package, and ran away.

A. Now you want to give the police a description of the muggers. Choose details that make them stand out—details that will help the police find them.

Person 1: _____

_____

_____

_____

Person 2: _____

_____

_____

_____

Some skilled artists need only draw a few lines to capture the qualities that make one person different from another. A lot of thought and practice are required to sort out these important details.

B. Take notes for a short character sketch of a person, real or fictional, that you know a lot about.

1. What is your main idea about the character? Is the person kind or wise or mean or funny or what?

_____

_____

_____

2. What are some outstanding details about the character's appearance?

_____

_____

_____

3. What are some outstanding details about how the person sounds or what the person says?

_____

_____

_____

4. What are some outstanding details about how the person behaves?

_____

_____

_____

Write On Select the most important details about the character you examined in part B. (You may find that you need still more.) Complete a brief character sketch in one or two paragraphs.

Details are important in character descriptions. When you describe a character, choose details that make that person special.

5 Describing the setting for a mystery

Why are mysteries so interesting? Often some details in the **setting**—the place where things happen—are not quite right. The reader senses that something strange is about to take place. Read the paragraph below.

> I didn't see why she was so upset. Everything looked normal to me. It was just an old room that had been closed up for a year. In the corner was an umbrella stand full of canes. On the walls were frames that held pictures of faded men and women. There were two plump armchairs, a lamp, a red sofa, and a radio whose dials looked like eyes. Janet came closer and said in a low voice, "I nailed that door shut before we left." A cold draft came through the opened doorway.

A. List two or three details that make the paragraph above seem mysterious.

_____

_____

_____

B. Tell about an indoor setting that you know well. In a paragraph, describe several details about that house or room. Don't make this description mysterious.

_____

_____

_____

_____

_____

_____

C. Describe the same setting again. This time, a mystery takes place there. Change or add some details. Make your reader pay attention and become a detective. (Everything is normal, except . . .)

_____

_____

_____

_____

_____

D. Now write a paragraph about an outdoor setting where a mystery takes place. If you like, make it a place you know.

_____

_____

_____

_____

_____

Write On Pick your best setting description above and have a character enter that setting. Your character may look or act quite normal, but there is something odd or mysterious about him or her. On a separate sheet, write two paragraphs. First, introduce the setting. Then introduce the character.

Mystery settings usually include unusual or strange details.

Revising

6 Choosing adverbs

John jumped.

A subject and verb form the backbone of every sentence. However, a subject and verb alone often leave questions in the reader's mind. Adverbs and adverbial phrases can answer these questions.

When? John jumped first . . . after the crash. . . .
Where? John jumped up . . . down . . . onto the deck . . . twenty-six feet. . . .
How? John jumped effortlessly . . . with fear in his eyes . . . awkwardly. . . .

A. Here is another simple sentence: *Chita cheered.* Expand it to answer the following questions.

When? Chita cheered _____.

Where? Chita cheered _____.

How? Chita cheered _____.

B. Now expand this sentence: *Harold sank.* This time answer each question in different ways.

When? Harold sank _____.

Harold sank _____.

Where? Harold sank _____.

Harold sank _____.

How? Harold sank _____.

Harold sank _____.

When and where? Harold sank _____

_____.

Where and how?   Harold sank _____

_____ .

Adverbs help verbs say more. However, you should be careful about overdoing adverbs. Some writers count on adverbs to do the job that a stronger verb could do by itself. Other writers add adverbs when their verbs are strong enough to stand by themselves. Both these practices should be avoided.

Wordy: Sally <u>went quickly</u> to the door.
Better: Sally <u>raced</u> to the door.
Wordy: Sally <u>ran quickly</u> to the door.
Better: Sally <u>ran</u> to the door. (The verb *ran* implies quickness.)

C. Rewrite the following sentences to eliminate unneeded adverbs. Where necessary, put strong verbs in place of weak verbs.

1. Ingrid looked angrily at Jim.

_____

2. The train sped rapidly into the tunnel.

_____

3. Jiro walked tiredly across the field.

_____

4. Rosemaria smiled cheerfully.

_____

5. "Hello," said Juan softly.

_____

Look over the "Write On" papers you have written for this unit. Check for writing that leaves the reader in doubt about when, where, and how things happen. Choose a paper that needs help and revise it, adding or deleting adverbs and changing verbs as necessary.

Use adverbs and adverbial phrases to tell when, where, and how. Do not use adverbs when a strong verb can do the job by itself, or when the verb already implies the meaning of the adverb.

Proofreading

lesson

7 Making subjects and verbs agree

Most verbs have two present-tense forms: the **plain form,** like *whistle,* and the **s form,** like *whistles.* The verb form must go with, or **agree** with, the subject. Follow the rules below for subject–verb agreement.

1. **Use the plain form with I, you, and plural subjects.**

   I whistle.   You whistle.
   The canaries whistle.   Jamie and Ben whistle.

2. **Use the s form with singular nouns and pronouns, including indefinite pronouns like someone and nobody.**

   The kettle whistles.   She whistles.
   Everybody whistles.

3. **The verb be has special forms for both present and past tense.**

   I am whistling.   He is whistling.   They are whistling.
   I was whistling.   He was whistling.   They were whistling.

4. **Some verbs change their spelling to make the s form.**

   do—does   have—has   carry—carries

A. Underline the correct form of the verb in each sentence that follows.

   1. I (was, were) looking at a strange photo.
   2. In it, a house (stand, stands) on top of a hill.
   3. The windows (is, are) all shuttered.
   4. A man and woman (sit, sits) on the porch.
   5. They (is, are) staring into a field.
   6. Nothing (seem, seems) to be there.
   7. I (wonder, wonders) who they (is, are).
   8. The photo (make, makes) me feel sad.

B. Change each past-tense sentence below to present tense. Be sure your subjects and verbs agree.

   1. Yesterday it rained.

      Now _____.

62

2. Yesterday we played cards.

   Now _____.

3. Yesterday Lori baked brownies.

   Now _____.

4. Yesterday Mark and Reginald made a salad.

   Now _____.

5. Yesterday everyone enjoyed lunch.

   Now _____.

C. Proofread and correct the paragraph below. Watch out for errors in punctuation, capitalization, and subject–verb agreement.

   The cowhand walks slowly down the dusty street he go past the lone star cafe rand's hotel and the first national bank nobody seem to be around suddenly two shots rings out

When you proofread your writing, check to see that your present-tense verbs agree with the subject. Follow the rules on page 62.

Post-Test

1. The encyclopedia entry below is a short biography of an inventor. Cross out the details that do not belong in a brief biography.

   Elmo Brainchild, born 1940, Genesee, NY. American inventor, attended Harvard University. Owns a pet cat and dog. Inventions include: a two-pronged toothpick, a pocket-sized popcorn popper, and high-protein bubblegum. He reads three newspapers a day and does the crossword puzzles. Works at the XK-5 Laboratory in Pittsburgh as senior inventor.

2. Write four details that describe a rose.

   _____

   _____

   _____

   _____

3. Write a paragraph of description using the sentence below as your topic sentence.

   Detective Hansen noticed a suspicious-looking man sitting alone in the restaurant.

4. Rewrite each sentence below. Use a more powerful verb so that the adverbs are no longer necessary.

   a. Erica asked the school earnestly to build a new gym.

   _____

   b. The accident happened to us unexpectedly.

   _____

   c. Kristen walked quickly away from the angry bull.

   _____

unit 5
Writing
Facts and Opinions

Things to Remember About Writing Facts and Opinions

A **fact** is a statement that can be tested or checked. An **opinion** expresses someone's feelings.

Writing Tips

- Use words like *hate, love, like, believe, think, best,* and *worse* when writing opinions.
- Write facts that answer the questions *who, what, where, why,* and *when* when writing news stories.
- Back up your opinions with facts to make them more convincing.

Revising Tips

- Make short, choppy sentences into a longer, smoother sentence by combining whole sentences or sentence parts.

Proofreading Tips

Check to see if you have
- used the correct past-tense forms of verbs
- used the correct participle forms after *has, have,* and *had*

1 Writing facts

"Nobody likes the metric system—and that's a fact."

But is it a fact? A **fact** is a statement that can be tested or checked to see if it's true. An **opinion,** on the other hand, expresses someone's feelings. Opinions often contain words like *hate, love, like, believe, think, best, worst.* The sentence about the metric system cannot be proved, so it is not a fact. It contains the word *like,* so it is an opinion. Since many scientists and citizens of other countries have used the metric system for a long time, the sentence isn't even accurate.

A. Write one fact about the metric system.

B. Each statement below is based on the picture. Five of the statements are accurate facts. Mark them *F*. Three statements are opinions. Mark them *O*. Two of the statements are clearly not accurate. Mark them *I*.

_____ 1. The dog is chasing the cat.

_____ 2. The thermometer reading is more than ninety degrees.

_____ 3. The vendor's ice-cream cones are too expensive.

_____ 4. The ice-cream cart is shaded by an umbrella.

_____ 5. The girl looks neat.

_____ 6. The boy is dressed in sloppy clothes.

_____ 7. The boy and girl are sitting on the steps.

_____ 8. The boy has a basketball.

_____ 9. The ice-cream vendor has a beard.

_____ 10. The store sells food.

C. Write five more facts—*only* facts—about the picture.

1. _____

2. _____

3. _____

4. _____

5. _____

Write On

On another sheet of paper, write two paragraphs about the picture. In one paragraph, include only facts. In the other, give opinions as well as facts. Try to base each paragraph on a main idea or topic sentence.

Facts can be tested or checked. Opinions express feelings and often contain words like <u>hate</u>, <u>love</u>, <u>like</u>, <u>believe</u>, <u>think</u>, <u>best</u>, and <u>worst</u>. Inaccurate statements can be disproved.

---

2 Writing news and feature stories

Suppose that you've just been made an editor of the school newspaper. You sent a new reporter out to report on a school basketball game, and this is the story the reporter turned in.

> The basketball team lost another game yesterday. The score wasn't even close. Some of the players I talked to feel that the coach isn't strict enough. People miss practice and still get to play in the game.
>
> This reporter feels that there should be stricter rules and more practice so that our team will start winning again.

A **news story** should stick to facts like the **five W's—Who? What? When? Where? Why?** A news reporter should not leave out important facts or include personal opinions in the story.

A. On the lines below, make a list of specific questions the reporter should answer in a news article reporting the basketball game. Think about the five W's.

_____

_____

_____

_____

B. Now make up answers for your questions from part **A.** On the lines below, write a short news story about the losing basketball game. Try to answer all five W's.

_____

_____

_____

_____

_____

_____

_____

Not all stories in newspapers are news stories. Sometimes papers print **feature stories.** Feature stories often spotlight a person in the news or give background information about an event. Feature stories may include opinions. For example, a feature story on the school basketball team might be an interview with the coach and some players on the team. Such a story would probably include a description of the attitudes and opinions of those being interviewed.

C. For each news headline below, suggest an idea for a feature story that would give readers additional information about the event.

1. **New Menu for School Cafeteria**

_____

2. **Student Wins National Spelling Bee**

_____

3. **Class Play Is Big Success**

_____

4. **Team Wins State Championship**

_____

Choose one of the news/feature pairs from part **C** or write a pair based on something that happened at your school. On a separate sheet of paper, write a news story and a feature story. Use real or made-up facts and, where appropriate, opinions.

News stories contain facts that answer the questions <u>who</u>, <u>what</u>, <u>where</u>, <u>when</u>, and <u>why</u>. Feature stories give additional background information on people and events, and they may contain opinions.

lesson

3 Writing about yourself

Have your ever filled out a form about yourself? Schools, government agencies, and businesses all have forms for people to complete.

A. Here is a form for you to fill in about yourself.

UNIVERSAL PERSON FORM (Please Print or Type)

Name _____
          (Last)   (First)   (Middle Initial)

Street Address _____

City or Town _____ **Telephone** _____

State _____ **Zip Code** _____

Date of Birth _____ **Place of Birth** _____

Names of Parents or Guardians _____

Names and Ages of Brothers and Sisters _____

_____

Height _____ **Weight** _____

Hair Color _____ **Eye Color** _____

Favorite Subject _____ **Favorite Hobby** _____

Last Book Read _____

Pets _____

Favorite Movie, Book, or TV Show _____

B. Most of the information asked for above is factual, but some categories are opinions. Put a star next to any opinions you wrote on the form.

70

When you write about your life, you are writing an **autobiography**. An autobiography includes facts, like those you listed on the form. But it includes more than just facts. A good autobiography tells what kind of person you are and what kind of person you hope to be.

C. One way to show what kind of person you are is to tell how you acted— what you said and did—during a specific event. A brief true story about yourself or someone else is called an **anecdote.** Write an anecdote about yourself on the lines below.

_____

_____

_____

_____

_____

_____

D. What are your hopes, dreams, and plans for the future? Write a few sentences below telling about them.

_____

_____

_____

_____

_____

Write On

On another sheet of paper, write a four-paragraph autobiography. The first paragraph should tell about your birth and early life; the second, about your school life. In the third paragraph, tell an anecdote that shows what kind of person you are. In the last paragraph, tell about your hopes and dreams for the future. Use the information you wrote for parts **A, C,** and **D.**

An autobiography is the story of your life. It includes both facts and opinions. Many autobiographies also include anecdotes and end by telling about plans for the future.

71

4 Writing a testimonial

It's intermission time on the Ricky Ticky Show, and look what's happening on the screen.

Here's what the people are saying:

Miss A: "I *love* Zappo!"
Mrs. B: "Zappo is *better!*"
Ms. C: "I couldn't get through the day without Zappo!"
Mr. D: "Zappo is double good!"
Mr. E: "Zappo is great!"

A. What facts do you know about Zappo now? What facts would you like to know?

_____

_____

_____

Ads about products usually contain many opinions but few facts. And consumers often need to know specific facts about cost, quality, and effectiveness before they buy a product.

B. Suppose that you were thinking about buying (a) an item of food, (b) an item of clothing, or (c) a piece of hobby equipment. Name the product you have in mind and write at least five questions you believe you should ask about it before making your purchase.

_____

_____

_____

_____

A **testimonial** is a statement about the excellence of a product or person. The best testimonials are based on facts.

C. Think of a product you have actually used with a great deal of satisfaction. Suppose that the manufacturer asks you for a testimonial of at least thirty words, telling _how_ and _why_ the product has been good for you. Write it here. Include specific facts, as well as your opinion.

_____

_____

_____

_____

_____

_____

Write On

Some people, like some products, deserve the praise they get. You're invited to speak at a testimonial dinner in honor of one of your favorite people. (The person can be real or imaginary.) Write a short speech giving the facts about why the person seems very special to you.

_____

Ads about products usually contain many opinions but few facts. However, a good testimonial about a person or product should be based on facts.

lesson 5 Writing a science fiction story

Darma strained her eyes to see the spaceship as it grew smaller, became just a speck against the yellow sky, and disappeared. She looked around warily at her new home. Then she straightened her shoulders and began to whistle. "Everything will be OK if I just keep my head," she decided.

The paragraph above is the beginning of a **science fiction story.** Science fiction deals with other worlds or with our world in another time—often the future. Science fiction stories may not be based on the facts as we know them, but a science fiction writer plans the setting, characters, and plot with care.

Science fiction **settings** are important. The writer may dream up a whole new world filled with unusual places that are carefully described.

A. Reread the paragraph about Darma. Then do the activities below.

1. Write what you already know about the setting.

_____

2. Add to the setting. Decide where Darma is. Give the place a name, and describe where it is and what it looks like.

_____

_____

_____

_____

_____

_____

Science fiction **characters** may be human beings or creatures from other worlds. They may look and act like us, or they may be completely different.

B. Think about what you learned about Darma—how she looks and feels. Decide who Darma is and describe her at the top of the next page. Then tell about one or two other characters she will meet in her new home.

Darma: _____

_____

_____

_____

Other Characters: _____

_____

_____

_____

Every story has a **plot.** Usually, a conflict or problem must be solved. Through a series of events, the plot builds to a **climax**—the exciting part where the conflict is solved—and then a **conclusion.**

C. Write a short outline for a plot about Darma and your other characters. Begin by telling why the spaceship left her. List other events, a climax, and a conclusion.

_____

_____

_____

_____

_____

_____

On another sheet of paper, write a science fiction story based on the setting, characters, and plot you described in parts **A, B,** and **C.**

Science fiction stories deal with other worlds or with our world in another time. They contain careful descriptions of setting, characters, and plot.

Revising

6 Combining sentences

Inexperienced writers often use short, choppy sentences. Combining sentences makes writing smoother, more varied, and more mature. There are many ways to combine sentences.

You can combine whole sentences or parallel parts of sentences by using the conjunctions *and, but,* or *or.* When you combine whole sentences, use a comma before the conjunction. Look at the examples below.

Whole Sentences: I looked for the ball. It wasn't there.
                   I looked for the ball, but it wasn't there.

Sentence Parts: Tony sighed. He shrugged his shoulders.
                   Tony sighed and shrugged his shoulders. (combined predicates)
                   The ball is in the bushes. It is under that car.
                   The ball is in the bushes or under that car. (combined adverbial phrases)

A. Use *and, but,* or *or* to combine each pair of sentences below.

1. We can play tennis. We can play chess.

_____

2. The day is sunny. The day is cool.

_____

3. Let's go outside. Let's enjoy the fine weather.

_____

4. Tony likes to play tennis. Bertha likes to play tennis.

_____

5. Tony doesn't play well. Bertha does.

_____

6. There are courts at the high school. There are courts in the park.

_____

Another way to combine sentences is to move words or word groups that follow a form of *be*. Look at these examples.

Adjective: That man is a reporter. He is <u>mild-mannered</u>.
              That mild-mannered man is a reporter.

Phrase: The helicopter is <u>on the roof</u>. It is falling.
              The helicopter on the roof is falling.

Noun Phrase: The man went into a revolving door. He is <u>a reporter</u>.
              The man, a reporter, went into a revolving door.

Notice that adjectives that follow a form of *be* are moved to a position in front of a noun. Modifying phrases are moved to a position after a noun. Noun phrases are moved to a position after a noun, and commas are placed around the noun phrase. We call this kind of noun phrase an **appositive.**

B. Combine each pair of sentences below. Use the examples above to help you.

1. The girl is on the helicopter. She works with the reporter.

_____

2. The reporter is a hero. He saves the helicopter.

_____

3. Their boss is the editor of the paper. He wants a story.

_____

4. The city is big. It is filled with villains.

_____

5. The home is under a railroad station. It belongs to one villain.

_____

Write On Look back at the "Write On" papers you've written in this unit. Do any have short, choppy sentences? Choose one paragraph to rewrite. Combine sentences where you can to make your paper smoother.

_____

You can sometimes combine two short, choppy sentences into one longer, smoother sentence.

_____

Proofreading

7 Using verb forms correctly

You know which present-tense forms to use to make subjects and verbs agree. Now follow the rules below to use other verb forms correctly.

1. **Add -d or -ed to most regular verbs to make past-tense forms. Verbs that end in y after a consonant change y to i before adding ed. Some verbs double the consonant before adding ed. These verbs have one syllable, or two syllables with the accent on the second syllable, and they end with one vowel followed by one consonant.**

   wonder—wonder<u>ed</u> scurry—scurr<u>ied</u> cram—cram<u>med</u>
   create—create<u>d</u>   tally—tall<u>ied</u>   regret—regret<u>ted</u>

2. **Some irregular verbs have the same form for the present and the past tense. You can check for irregular past-tense forms in your dictionary.**

   quit—<u>quit</u>   hurt—<u>hurt</u>   shut—<u>shut</u>

3. **Other irregular verbs form their past tense in various ways. Check your dictionary.**

   blow—<u>blew</u>   ring—<u>rang</u>   think—<u>thought</u>
   take—<u>took</u>   buy—<u>bought</u>   go—<u>went</u>

A. Fill in the correct past-tense form for each verb below. Use a dictionary if you need help.

1. refer _____ 6. undertake _____

2. overcome _____ 7. notify _____

3. seek _____ 8. put _____

4. pay _____ 9. rebuild _____

5. write _____ 10. spread _____

4. **The participle form of a verb is used after has, have, or had. For regular verbs, the participle form is the same as the past form.**

   have <u>wondered</u>   had <u>scurried</u>   has <u>regretted</u>

5. The participle forms of irregular verbs are often different from past-tense forms. Check your dictionary.

has <u>blown</u>   had <u>rung</u>   have <u>taken</u>

B. Write in the correct form of the verb in parentheses for each sentence below. Use a dictionary if you need help.

1. How had the thief ——————— the painting?   (steal)

2. How could anyone have ——————— into a locked room?   (get)

3. No one had ——————— anything.   (see)

4. No one had ——————— any noises.   (hear)

5. The painting had ——————— Countess Smirkov a fortune.   (cost)

6. She had ——————— a guard dog.   (buy)

7. Only she ——————— how to open the lock.   (know)

8. Yet someone had ——————— it.   (do)

9. Someone had ——————— the painting.   (take)

10. So she ——————— to Homelock Sherles.   (write)

When you proofread your writing, check to see if:
- **you used correct past-tense forms**
- **you used correct participle forms after <u>has</u>, <u>have</u>, and <u>had</u>**

Use the rules on these pages to help you.

Post-Test

1. Read the following paragraph. Then answer the question below the paragraph.

   The students at Forsyth Elementary School have changed Bear Park from a wasteland into a flourishing garden. The energetic youngsters have carted away garbage, cleaned walks, and planted shrubs. The leader of the clean-up campaign is Amy Jong, a warm, cheerful eighth-grader.

   Is the paragraph part of a news story or a feature story? Give a reason for your answer.

   _____

2. Put a check next to the testimonial that sounds more convincing. Then give a reason for your choice.

   a. _____ Colson's Oven Cleaner has changed my life. I used to dread cleaning ovens but now it's my greatest joy in life. Thank you, Colson Cleaning Company!

   b. _____ Colson's Oven Cleaner is an inexpensive, non-toxic cleaning fluid that really works. It dissolves burnt grease quickly and doesn't smell as horrible as most oven cleaners.

   Explain your choice. _____

3. Write a brief anecdote about yourself, a friend, or a family member.

4. Combine each pair of sentences below.

   a. Jon and Frank play practical jokes. They are identical twins.

   _____

   b. Isis won first prize at the Chicago Cat Show. Isis is a Siamese cat.

   _____

   c. The car had a tape deck and stereo speakers. The car was new.

   _____

unit 6
Writing About Cause and Effect

Things to Remember When Writing About Cause and Effect

A **cause** tells why something happens. An **effect** is what happens.

Writing Tips

- Use words and phrases like *because, consequently, as a result,* and *therefore* to connect ideas in cause-and-effect writing.
- Use a series of causes and effects to lead to the solution of a problem in a story.
- Tell about the causes of the conflict and resolution when writing a story.

Revising Tips

- Use subordinate conjunctions and relative pronouns to combine short, choppy sentences into a longer, smoother sentence.

Proofreading Tips

Check to see that you have

- used quotation marks around a direct quotation
- set off the quotation from the rest of the sentence with a comma, a question mark, or an exclamation point
- capitalized the first word of the quotation

Using cause and effect words

What's going on here? Look at the picture and read the description below.

A woman was hit by an egg on Main Street yesterday. Paint fell on a man's head. A dog chased a cat. A juggler messed up his act. A man fell on the sidewalk. A ladder tipped over. A woman thought it was raining and opened her umbrella. A painter fell into a puddle.

Why did these things happen? The story would be much more interesting if these **effects** and their **causes** were connected. If a writer uses words and phrases like *because*, *therefore*, *as a result*, or *consequently*, the story will make more sense.

A. Write your own description of what's happening in the picture. Use some cause-and-effect words to make things clear.

_____

_____

_____

_____

_____

B. Use each sentence below as a cause. Connect it to an effect sentence by using the word in parentheses. Write both sentences on the line provided.

1. Jill bumped into the easel.   (since)

_____

2. Bill stayed up all night.   (consequently)

_____

3. Andrea smiled at Cliff.   (as a result)

_____

C. Use each sentence below as an effect. Connect it to a cause sentence. Use your own cause-and-effect word. Write both sentences on the line provided.

1. The fender was bent.

_____

2. Grandpa jumped into the lake.

_____

3. I failed my math test.

_____

Write On

You have many skills. Most of them are learned. Write a paragraph about something you're really good at. Explain the cause or causes of your skill.

Words and phrases like <u>because</u>, <u>consequently</u>, <u>as a result</u>, and <u>therefore</u> are often used to connect ideas in cause-and-effect writing.

2 Writing a story conflict and resolution

The two pictures below show the makings of a short story.

A. On the lines below, write a mini-story. Tell what's happening in each picture and why.

_____

_____

_____

_____

_____

Professional writers sometimes think of the short story as a simple matter of **conflict** (problems, dangers, competition) and **resolution**—settling the conflict.

One writer has said, "You get your characters into trouble, and then you get them out." It's not that simple, of course. If it were, a story about the two pictures on page 84 might be:

> Lester and Mary had hated each other all their lives. Then they became good friends.

That's not very interesting or informative. What more is needed? For one thing, the reader wants to know about the causes of the conflict and resolution. The events in a story are often a series of causes and effects that lead to a solution.

B. Here are five super-short stories (conflict plus resolution) which need to grow. Choose one. Use it as part of your outline for a longer story. Write your outline on the blanks below. List at least five events in a cause-and-effect chain.

1. I was accused of stealing the money.
   I proved I was innocent.
2. Jennie and I were the two finalists.
   She won.
3. I stood at the edge of the cliff, poisonous snakes on either side of me and an angry tiger in front of me.
   Quick thinking saved my life.
4. "I can't trust you," said Armando's father.
   Armando and his father shook hands, friends again.

_____

_____

_____

_____

_____

_____

Write On In part **B,** you wrote an outline for a story. On a separate paper, write the story. Include dialogue and details to bring your story to life. (You may want to read Lesson 7, pages 94 and 95, before you write dialogue.)

Many short stories contain a conflict and a resolution. A series of causes and effects often leads to the solution.

3 Writing about social studies

A. What's happening in the sequence of pictures below? Write a story to go with the pictures.

_____

_____

_____

_____

_____

_____

It's often been said that truth is stranger than fiction. Real-life events can be as exciting and dramatic as anything a writer can make up.

B. You've just written about a conflict—and its causes—that is really happening in many parts of the country. Now continue the story. Write about a resolution, or a possible resolution, of the conflict.

_____

_____

_____

Social studies is full of interesting "short stories," past and present. Here are just a few brief examples:

History
Conflict: Christopher Columbus is mocked because of his ideas.
Resolution: Queen Isabella provides funds for his voyage.

Geography
Conflict: Hurricanes cause huge losses in life and property.
Resolution: Scientists work to improve "early warning" systems.

Current Events
Conflict: Two nations fight over territory.
(Possible) Resolution: United Nations sends peacekeeping force into disputed area.

C. Write a brief outline of two social studies "short stories" that interest you.

1. Conflict: _____

   Resolution: _____

2. Conflict: _____

   Resolution: _____

Write On

Pick one of the social studies story outlines you wrote for part C. Complete a short report. Remember to include the causes of the conflict and the causes of the resolution.

_____

In social studies, a writer can often tell about events in a conflict-and-resolution format.

_____

Writing a letter of complaint

45 Elm Place
Center City
March 4, 19–

President
Frammis Manufacturing Co.
12 Main Street
Center City

Dear President:

I'm mad! I bought an "unbreak-able" Frammis. Well, it broke. What's the matter with your company? I think you make lousy products. People trust your advertising slogans, and what do they get? Junk! I'll never buy your stuff again. I want my money back. If I don't get satis-faction, I guarantee you there will be trouble.

Sincerely yours,
Ann Gree

13 Oak Lane
Center City
March 4, 19–

President
Frammis Manufacturing Co.
12 Main Street
Center City

Dear President:

On March 1, I bought a deluxe, high-speed Frammis, model number 33D, at the BG Hardware Store in my town. The third time I used my Frammis, the left ejector bolt broke. This made my Frammis unusable. Since the Frammis is advertised as "unbreakable," I would like it re-placed with one that works properly.

Sincerely yours,
Cora Calmer

A. Compare the two letters of complaint above. Which one do you think is more effective? Why?

_____

_____

_____

_____

No matter how angry a buyer may be, it often helps to explain how and why things happened. A **letter of complaint** should tell the causes of the problem and suggest a method of resolving it.

Suppose that the events shown above happened to you.

B. Complete the body of the complaint letter below. Tell the causes of your complaint and suggest a resolution.

On May 14, I bought a Sweetsound Record Player at the Acme Music Store.

_____

_____

_____

_____

_____

Write On

Think of an unsatisfactory product you bought or a bad situation in your school, neighborhood, or town. On another sheet of paper, write a letter of complaint to a company, school, or local official. List causes and suggest a resolution. Turn to page 110 for the correct letter style.

A letter of complaint should list causes for the complaint and suggest a solution to the problem.

5 Writing a myth

Why are there thunder and lightning in the sky? Here's one sort of explanation.

> The ruler of all the gods was called Zeus. He lived in the clouds on top of Mount Olympus, the highest mountain in Greece. His weapon was a bolt of lightning. He threw the bolt to frighten his enemies. When lightning flashed across the sky, it was caused by Zeus's anger. The rolling of his chariot caused the sound we call thunder.

The paragraph above tells about a **myth.** Thousands of years ago, many people used myths to explain how the world worked. They believed that the forces of nature and their own actions were controlled by various gods, super-people, and superanimals.

A. What really causes lightning and thunder? Write a short scientific explanation on the lines below.

_____

_____

_____

_____

_____

B. Write a short outline for a myth of your own invention. Your myth should explain one of the following topics (or another one of your own choice):

Why the grass is green   Why earthquakes happen
Why the sky is blue   Why some trees are always green
Why the wind blows   Why people grow old
Why the rain falls   Why dogs are friendly to humans

_____

_____

_____

_____

_____

_____

Write On Once you are satisfied with your basic idea for a myth, write it on another sheet of paper. Remember to keep cause and effect very clear.

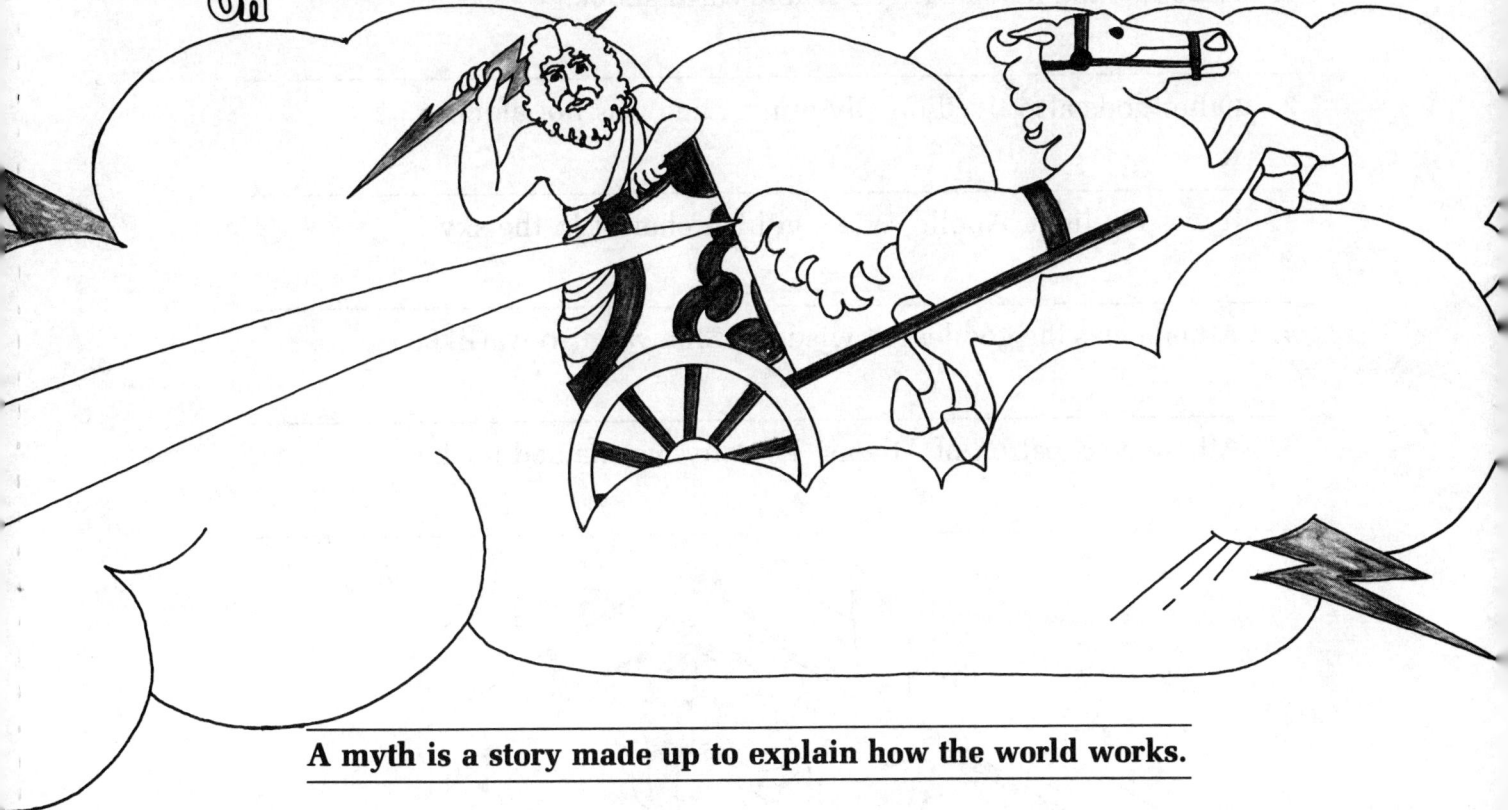

A myth is a story made up to explain how the world works.

Revising

More about combining sentences

You know that you can combine sentences by using the conjunctions *and*, *but*, or *or*. But the relationship between two sentences can often be shown more clearly by using a **subordinate conjunction**, such as *if* or *when*. Look at the examples below:

> Zeus threw his lightning bolt. The sky lit up.
> Zeus threw his lightning bolt<u>, and</u> the sky lit up.
> <u>When</u> Zeus threw his lightning bolt<u>,</u> the sky lit up.

Subordinate conjunctions often show cause-and-effect or time relationships between the sentences being combined. Some subordinate conjunctions that show cause and effect are *because*, *since*, *if*, *so*, *although*, and *unless*. Some subordinate conjunctions that show time are *when*, *before*, *after*, and *while*.

A. Combine each pair of sentences below. Try to use a different subordinate conjunction in each sentence.

1. Zeus nodded his head. The whole earth shook.

    _____

2. Other gods also lived on Olympus. Zeus was not alone.

    _____

3. It was daylight. Apollo rode a golden chariot in the sky.

    _____

4. Athena was the goddess of wisdom. She was also warlike.

    _____

5. Athena was patron of Athens. The city was named for her.

    _____

Another way to combine sentences is to use a **relative pronoun,** like *who, which,* or *that.* Look at these examples.

Apollo and Artemis were twins. They were gods of the sun and moon.
Apollo and Artemis, who were twins, were gods of the sun and moon.
Apollo and Artemis, who were gods of the sun and moon, were twins.

Artemis hunted wild beasts. The beasts lived in the mountains.
Artemis hunted wild beasts that lived in the mountains.

Relative pronouns can be used when the same noun (or a pronoun that stands for it) appears in both sentences. The relative pronoun is used to replace one noun. Then the sentence with the relative pronoun is inserted into the other sentence. Notice that if the same noun is the subject of both sentences, either subject can be replaced with a relative pronoun and inserted into the other sentence. See the first example above.

B. Combine each pair of sentences below. Use either a relative pronoun or a subordinate conjunction—whichever you think fits better.

1. Hermes was the messenger of the gods. He lived on Olympus.

_____

2. He wore winged sandals. They carried him over land and sea.

_____

3. Hermes ran on the sunbeams. The sunbeams sloped down to earth.

_____

4. Mortal eyes were too weak to see him. Hermes came in dreams.

_____

5. There are many Greek myths. The myths tell about the gods.

_____

6. We can still enjoy the myths. They are good stories.

_____

Look back at the "Write On" papers you've written for this unit. Try to combine any short, choppy sentences by using subordinate conjunctions or relative pronouns. Rewrite your paragraph on a separate sheet of paper.

_____

Use subordinate conjunctions and relative pronouns to combine short sentences.

_____

Proofreading

7

Writing dialogue correctly

Your story and its characters will come to life when you include **dialogue,** or conversation. The exact words someone says are called a **direct quotation.** Read this short dialogue.

"How could you have spilled ink on my class project?" Mary asked angrily.

"I didn't mean to do it. It happened when Vic hit my arm," Lester replied.

Mary snapped, "That's no excuse."

Follow these rules for writing dialogue.

1. **Start and end each quotation with quotation marks.**
2. **Begin a new paragraph for each new speaker.**
3. **Capitalize the first word of a quotation.**
4. **Set off a quotation from the rest of the sentence with a comma, a question mark, or an exclamation point. A section of direct quotation ends with a period only when it is the end of the sentence.** (See the last sentence in the sample dialogue.)

A. Read these sentences carefully. Add the missing punctuation marks in each one. Use the sample and rules on page 94 to help you.

1. How does your leg feel now that the cast is off Doctor Mehdi asked.

2. Tillie replied Much better now, Doctor.

3. You'll need the crutches for only another week or two the doctor added.

4. But will I be able to tap dance Tillie asked eagerly.

5. Yes, of course smiled Doctor Mehdi.

6. How wonderful! I never could before I broke my leg beamed Tillie.

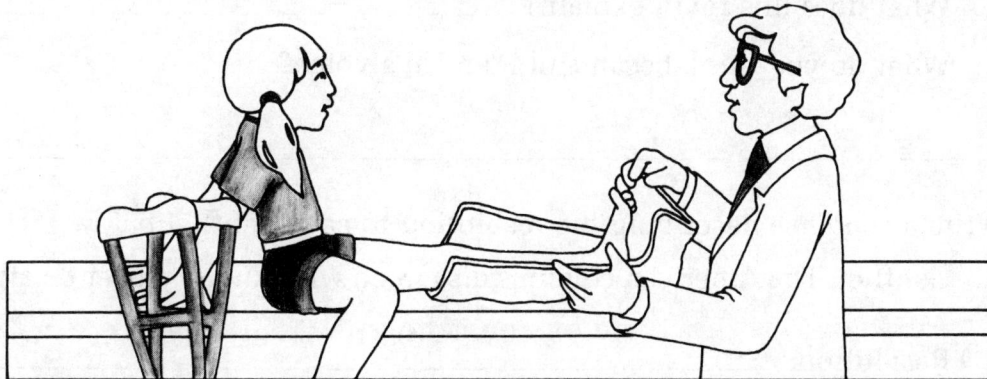

B. Choose one of the pictures in this unit. On the lines below, write a short dialogue between two characters in the picture.

_____

_____

_____

_____

_____

_____

When you proofread your writing, check to see if
- **you used quotation marks around a direct quotation**
- **you set off the quotation from the rest of the sentence with a comma, a question mark, or an exclamation point**
- **you capitalized the first word of the quotation**

1. A Chinese myth tells about P'an Ku, a man who lived 18,000 years. Read about P'an Ku below and answer the questions that follow.

    After P'an Ku established the universe, he died. His breath became the wind, his blood turned into rivers, his hair turned into trees and plants, and his bones became rocks.

    a. What does this myth explain? _____

    b. What do you think became of P'an Ku's voice?

    _____

2. Write a sentence describing the resolution to each conflict below.

    a. Conflict: The American colonies disagreed with England over taxation.

        Resolution: _____

    b. Conflict: Many people found it difficult to pay their high heating bills.

        Resolution: _____

3. James Thurber wrote about a funny sequence of events in "The Night the Bed Fell." Write a paragraph describing what happens when your bed suddenly collapses during the night. Describe at least four effects.

4. Combine each pair of sentences below. Use relative pronouns or subordinate conjunctions.

    a. The map led up to the treasure. The map was very old.

        _____

    b. Tammy couldn't play softball. She broke her leg.

        _____

    c. Nina speaks Spanish and English. Nina was born in Ecuador.

        _____

unit 7
Making Your Point in Writing

Things to Remember About Making Your Point in Writing

The **purpose** of a piece of writing may be to inform, to entertain, to express feelings or opinions, or to persuade.

Writing Tips
- Know your purpose before you begin to write.
- Base your opinions on facts in order to write persuasively.
- Include as many facts as possible.
- Base your editorials and letters to the editor of a newspaper on facts. Offer clear solutions to the problem discussed.

Revising Tips
- Correct any misplaced modifiers or dangling modifiers.

Proofreading Tips Check that you have
- used apostrophes in possessives and contractions
- written the six parts of a business letter correctly

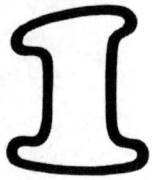

1 Writing persuasively

A. Read each paragraph below. Then answer the questions that follow.

☐ People eat too much junk food. It's not good to do that. In fact, it's really dumb. People should eat better.

☐ People eat too much junk food. Nutritionists agree that a well-balanced diet should include fruits, vegetables, and grains. Most prepared foods contain sugar and artificial ingredients that have little nutritional value. Before people eat packaged foods, they should read the labels. Perhaps then they would replace junk snacks with fruits, nuts, and cheese.

1. Put an X in the box of the paragraph you think is more persuasive.
2. Explain why you think that paragraph is more persuasive.

_____

_____

_____

_____

_____

In order to persuade someone of something, base your opinion on **facts.** The more facts you include, the more persuasive your writing will probably be.

B. Suppose that you're on the committee to pick new uniforms for a school band. Look at the pictures of the two types being considered. Then answer the questions below.

1. List as many facts as you can about each uniform.

    Uniform 1: _____

    _____

    _____

    Uniform 2: _____

    _____

    _____

2. Now write your opinion for the uniform committee meeting. Make it as persuasive as you can.

    _____

    _____

    _____

    _____

    _____

    _____

Write On

Choose one of the topics below or one you like better. On a separate sheet, list facts to support each side of the argument. Which side seems right to you? Choose that side, and write a persuasive paragraph to support the argument.

TV viewing has a good (bad) influence on young people.
The Equal Rights Amendment should (should not) be passed.
Capital punishment helps (does not help) prevent crime.
Baseball should (should not) be called the national sport.

To write persuasively, base your opinions on facts. Include as many facts as you can.

2 Writing for a specific audience

A. Look at the picture and answer the questions below.

1. Do you think the people are enjoying the speech? Why or why not?

_____

_____

2. Put a check mark next to the topics below that you think the Centerville Dog Lovers would enjoy hearing about.

_____ How Dogs Are Our Best Friends

_____ Scientific Experiments with Rats

_____ The Joys of Raising Cats

_____ How to Teach an Old Dog New Tricks

A speaker or writer must keep in mind the **audience** who will be listening or reading. Some topics will appeal only to certain audiences. For example, "The Growing Season in Iceland" might interest Icelandic farmers, but would hardly be of interest to most Americans.

Even a topic of general interest requires different kinds of information presented differently, depending on the knowledge and interests of the audience. You can write more technically for those who know a lot about a topic. But you need to write quite simply for those who know only a little.

B. Check the topics below that you think a group of first-graders would be interested in hearing about.

_____ Zoo Animals   _____ College Scholarships

_____ The Income Tax   _____ Kite Flying

_____ Why Snow Falls   _____ Weather in Indonesia

C. Circle the words below that you would probably _not_ use in writing for, or speaking to, first-graders.

bird	money	extraordinary
species	aeronautical	hot
exemption	fly	meterology

D. Write a short paragraph on one of the topics you choose for part **B.** Write for a first-grade audience.

_____

_____

_____

_____

_____

On a separate paper, write about your favorite sport or hobby. First write an article for a magazine meant for fellow players or hobbyists. Then describe the sport or hobby in a letter to your pen pal from Mars.

When you write, keep in mind the audience for whom you are writing.

3 Writing an advertisement

New, exciting, fun—that's a Wellabee!

Basketball star Joe Giraffi says, "I love my Wellabee!"

Don't be left out! Join the happy crowds who are getting a new Wellabee!

A. Read the ads above and answer the questions below.

1. What words does the first ad use to describe a Wellabee?

   _____

2. What does the second ad do to interest you in a Wellabee?

   _____

3. How does the third ad try to appeal to you?

   _____

4. Do any of the ads give you facts about a Wellabee?

   _____

   Ad writers try to persuade you to buy their product by using different methods. They may use **loaded words,** like *wonderful* and *great,* to make the product sound good. They may use a **famous person** who says he or she likes the product. They may use the **bandwagon method**—saying everyone else is doing it and you should "jump on the bandwagon" too.

   The device shown here is a Freebixer. It costs $16.95, and it is guaranteed to operate properly for five years.

THE ORIGINAL FREEBIXER ONLY $16.95

B. What does a Freebixer do? Anything you want it to. Perhaps it repairs flammuses and gibblegaws. Perhaps it will walk your dog or guard your bike. Invent the facts about your Freebixer and write them here.

_____

_____

_____

C. Write an ad that will persuade others to want to buy and own a Freebixer. Include at least two of the methods described on page 102.

_____

_____

_____

_____

Did the Wellabee ads give any facts about the product? Did your ad give any facts about the Freebixer? Today many people look for facts before they will buy a product.

D. Rewrite your ad, paying more attention to facts. But don't forget to appeal to your readers' feelings as well.

_____

_____

_____

_____

Write On

Suppose that you are (a) seeking an after-school job or (b) running for a class office. On another sheet of paper, write an advertisement for yourself, designed to persuade the reader to choose you.

Ads often use loaded words, famous people, and the bandwagon method to persuade readers. But ads should also include facts.

Writing an editorial

Newspapers are mostly filled with facts. One place in which opinions are appropriate is the editorial page. An **editorial** is an article that presents the opinion of the editor or editorial staff of the paper. Editorials are often written about local or national problems and offer solutions.

It's ten o'clock on Monday morning. You're the editor of the local afternoon newspaper. As you think about ideas for today's editorials, you look out your office window onto this Main Street scene.

A. List three possible titles for the editorial you'll write today.

1. _____

2. _____

3. _____

B. Here are several more facts about your town. Read each one. Then write your final choice of an editorial topic. Check the boxes of the facts you will use in your editorial.

☐ Main Street trash collections are made every Tuesday, Thursday, and Saturday.
☐ Town laws forbid the posting of ads on light poles.
☐ The local police department has the lowest pay scale in the state. Forty jobs on the force have gone unfilled for months.
☐ The local power company is working on a two-year program to replace old light poles with new ones.
☐ Double parking or standing is against the law.

Your Editorial Topic: _____

C. Now write a one-paragraph editorial. Make sure that it is based on the facts, that it states the problem clearly, and that it offers a clear solution.

_____

_____

_____

_____

_____

_____

_____

Write On The editorial page also contains letters to the editor from citizens giving their opinions. On another sheet of paper, write a brief letter to the editor of your local paper about a problem in your neighborhood or school. Suggest a solution.

An editorial gives the opinion of the newspaper's editorial staff. Editorials should be based on facts and should offer clear solutions for the problem discussed.

---

lesson

5 Writing humor

What makes you laugh? A **pun** is one kind of humor. A pun uses a word which sounds like another word but has a different meaning. In *Through the Looking Glass*, Alice has the following conversation with the Red and White Queens. Read it and look for puns. It begins when the Red Queen asks Alice this question.

"How is bread made?"

"I know *that!*" Alice cried eagerly. "You take some flour—"

"Where do you pick the flower?" the White Queen asked. "In a garden or in the hedges?"

"Well, it isn't *picked* at all," Alice explained, "it's ground—"

"How many acres of ground?" said the Queen. "You mustn't leave out so many things."

—Lewis Carroll

A. Explain the two puns in the selection above. List the words and meanings being played with.

_____

_____

_____

_____

B. On the lines that follow, try making up a humorous conversation about the zoo. Use some of these words as puns.

bear (animal)—bear (carry)   horns (antlers)—horns (cars')
trunk (elephant's)—trunk (suitcase)   yak (animal)—yak (chatter)
seal (animal)—seal (fasten)   terns (birds)—turns (rotates)

_____

_____

_____

_____

Some jokes and riddles play with the meanings of word groups rather than single words.

What's a way to avoid falling hair?
Jump out of the way.

C. Try to think of funny answers to twist the meanings of these questions.

1. May I try on the dress in the window?

_____

2. What is this fly doing in my soup?

_____

3. How can I get ahead?

_____

Humor also comes from the unexpected or inappropriate. In a comedy, if a poorly dressed person gets hit with a pie, it isn't as funny as if a well-dressed person does. On the other hand, a person in rags getting into a fancy car might be humorous.

Use the picture below or your own ideas to write a humorous short story. Try to include some puns, jokes, and unexpected happenings.

Puns and some jokes play with the meanings of words. Humor also comes from the unexpected or inappropriate.

Placing modifiers correctly

You know that several short, choppy sentences can often be combined into one longer, smoother sentence. Look at these sentences.

> The committee met. It met in the principal's office. It met on Saturday. It met to plan a dance.

These short sentences would probably sound better if they were combined. But suppose they are combined into this sentence.

> The committee met to plan a dance in the principal's office on Saturday.

A. Answer the questions below about the sentence above.

1. What is wrong with the sentence?

_____

2. How would you revise it?

_____

Modifiers like "in the principal's office" and "on Saturday" need to be placed as close as possible to the words they modify. Otherwise they are **misplaced modifiers.** Look at these examples.

Misplaced: There is the book that I read on the second shelf.
Revised: There on the second shelf is the book that I read.

B. Each sentence below has a misplaced modifier. Rewrite each so that it makes better sense.

1. A bus will pick up students for the field trip in front of the school.

   _____

2. The police officer directed traffic wearing white gloves.

   _____

3. The man in the office with a beard is Doctor Ramirez.

   _____

4. My sister is the girl in the park on a swing.

   _____

Sometimes the writer combines sentences but leaves out important words. Modifying phrases are included, but the word they modify is left out. The modifier then dangles. Here is a **dangling modifier** and its revision.

Dangling: After rinsing the glasses, the dishwasher was turned on.
Revised: After rinsing the glasses, I turned on the dishwasher.

C. Revise each sentence below to remove the dangling modifier. You will have to add a word for the modifier to modify.

1. Walking in the playground, the bell rang.

   _____

2. Running down the street, my nose practically froze.

   _____

3. After enjoying an early breakfast, the sun came up.

   _____

4. While waiting in line, the last ticket was sold.

   _____

Write On

Look over the "Write On" papers you have written for this unit. Check for misplaced or dangling modifiers. Check to see if you can combine any short, choppy sentences. Choose one paper and revise it.

Check your writing to be sure that you have no misplaced or dangling modifiers.

Proofreading

Writing and punctuating business letters

Heading → 29 Beeper Street
Clink, Missouri
October 5, 19-

Inside → Editor
Address Daily Trumpet
Main Street
Clink, Missouri

Greeting → Dear Editor:

Body → Can't anyone stop the noise of midnight garbage pickups? The noise of one can's clanking is bad enough, but several collectors' shouts and laughter besides are deafening. I say collect the trash during the day or not at all.

Closing → Yours truly,
Signature → *Sy Lent*
Sy Lent

A. Read the **business letter** above and answer the following questions.

1. Name the six parts of a business letter.

_____   _____   _____

_____   _____   _____

2. Where are commas placed in the letter?

_____

_____

3. Where is there a colon?

_____

4. Where are apostrophes used?

_____

Use an apostrophe to show where a letter or letters are omitted in a **contraction:**

I'll—I will   she's—she is   won't—will not   didn't—did not

Use an apostrophe and *s* to make a singular noun or a plural noun that doesn't end in *s* into a **possessive.** Use only an apostrophe to make a plural noun that ends in *s* into a possessive.

one girl's coat, two girls' coats   one child's toy, the children's toys

B. Put in punctuation marks where they are needed below.

1. Pueblo Colorado
2. Your cousin
   Stanley

3. Isnt Marshas new jacket super?
4. We cant find the players
   uniforms.

C. Write a short letter to the editor in response to Sy Lent's letter.

_____

_____

_____

_____

_____

_____

_____

_____

_____

_____

Use apostrophes in possessives and contractions. Check to see that you have written the six parts of a business letter correctly.

Post-Test

1. Read the ad below. Underline the loaded words.

    Let's face facts. You love your dog, but he's got that . . . doggy breath! Next time, don't turn pale—turn to Stayle, the only mouthwash for dogs! Stayle has a rose sweet, springtime scent with the fresh, clean flavor that you and your dog will love!

2. Put a check next to the opinion that is more persuasive.

    a. _____ The play *All or Nothing* lived up to its name—it was nothing. The only people who didn't walk out were already fast asleep.

    b. _____ *All or Nothing* was a play about unbelievable characters trapped in an absurd plot. Even a talented cast couldn't make the dull dialogue come to life.

3. Suppose you are writing an article for *Bike* Magazine. Check the topics that might interest the magazine's readers.

    a. _____ The History of Vermont   c. _____ The Best Bikes for Touring

    b. _____ A Bike Tour in Vermont   d. _____ Cars of the Future

4. Write a paragraph persuading your school to give free parachuting lessons.

5. Rewrite each sentence, fixing the dangling modifiers.

    a. Quacking shrilly, Martha fed the ducks.

    _____

    b. After tossing and turning all night, Stan's eyes looked tired.

    _____

    c. Racing for the school bus, my books and papers fell on the ground.

    _____

unit 8

Point of View in Writing

Things to Remember About Point of View in Your Writing

A **point of view** is the way someone sees, thinks, or feels about something.

Writing Tips

- Decide on your point of view before you begin writing.
- Choose the writing form that best expresses your point of view: play, poem, short story, essay, or news article.
- Use a first-person narrator when you want to put yourself "inside" a character you have created.
- Use a third-person point of view when you want to include several viewpoints.

Revising and Proofreading Tips

Check that your writing

- says exactly what you want it to say
- is free from grammatical and mechanical errors

1

Using different writing forms

Suppose you're walking down the street one afternoon and come upon this surprising scene.

Each person in the picture has a **point of view**—a way of thinking and feeling—about the scene. And each person might use a different form of writing to write about the scene. You probably know that poems, plays, stories, essays, and news articles are all different writing forms.

A. List three people from the scene and the forms in which you think each might write.

Writer	Form
1. _____	_____
2. _____	_____
3. _____	_____

A **poem** uses rhythm and often rhyme to help express meaning. Poems often contain similes, metaphors, and other word pictures that describe a scene or feeling.

B. If you were a poet describing the scene, what word pictures would you use? On the lines below, write the beginning of a description of the scene as a poet might see it.

_____

_____

_____

_____

_____

C. Choose another writer that you listed in part **A.** Write a short description as that person might write it.

_____

_____

_____

_____

_____

Pick a simple scene (like snow falling) or a brief event (like the winning shot in a basketball game). Examine your topic from the points of view of two different people. On a separate paper, capture the two points of view in two different writing forms, one for each person.

_____

Each person who views a scene has a point of view. People may use different writing forms to express their points of view.

2 Changing writing forms

Here are some words that most Americans know.

> Oh, beautiful for spacious skies,
>   For amber waves of grain,
> For purple mountain majesties
>   Above the fruited plain!
> America! America!
>   God shed His grace on thee,
> And crown thy good with brotherhood,
>   From sea to shining sea.
>
> —*Katherine Lee Bates*

A. Can you express the same ideas as the first verse of "America the Beautiful" in a different writing form? Write a short essay expressing the same feelings.

_____

_____

_____

_____

_____

_____

_____

_____

_____

_____

Here is a short excerpt from a story called "The Cat and the Pain Killer."

One of the reasons why Tom's mind had drifted away from its secret troubles was that it had found a new and weighty matter to interest itself about. Becky Thatcher had stopped coming to school. Tom had struggled with his pride a few days and tried to "whistle her down the wind," but failed. He began to find himself hanging around her father's house, nights, and feeling very miserable. She was ill. What if she should die! There was distraction in the thought. He no longer took an interest in war, nor even in piracy. The charm of life was gone; there was nothing but dreariness left.

—Mark Twain

B. On the lines below, write a poem expressing how Tom felt about Becky Thatcher's illness.

_____

_____

_____

_____

_____

_____

Write On

Is it true that poetry is all around us? See if you can find some by rewriting the prose words of an advertisement, a cereal box blurb, a matchbook cover, street signs, or other familiar messages.

You can express similar ideas in different writing forms.

3 Writing a first-person narrative

Every story has an author. The author decides from whose point of view the story will be told, or **narrated.** If you are writing a story about yourself, you will probably use the **first-person pronouns**—*I, me, my,* and so on. This kind of story is called a **first-person narrative.**

A. Write a **narrative**—a straightforward telling of events—describing an interesting ten minutes or so in the past twenty-four hours of your life. Use first-person pronouns.

_____

_____

_____

_____

_____

_____

_____

_____

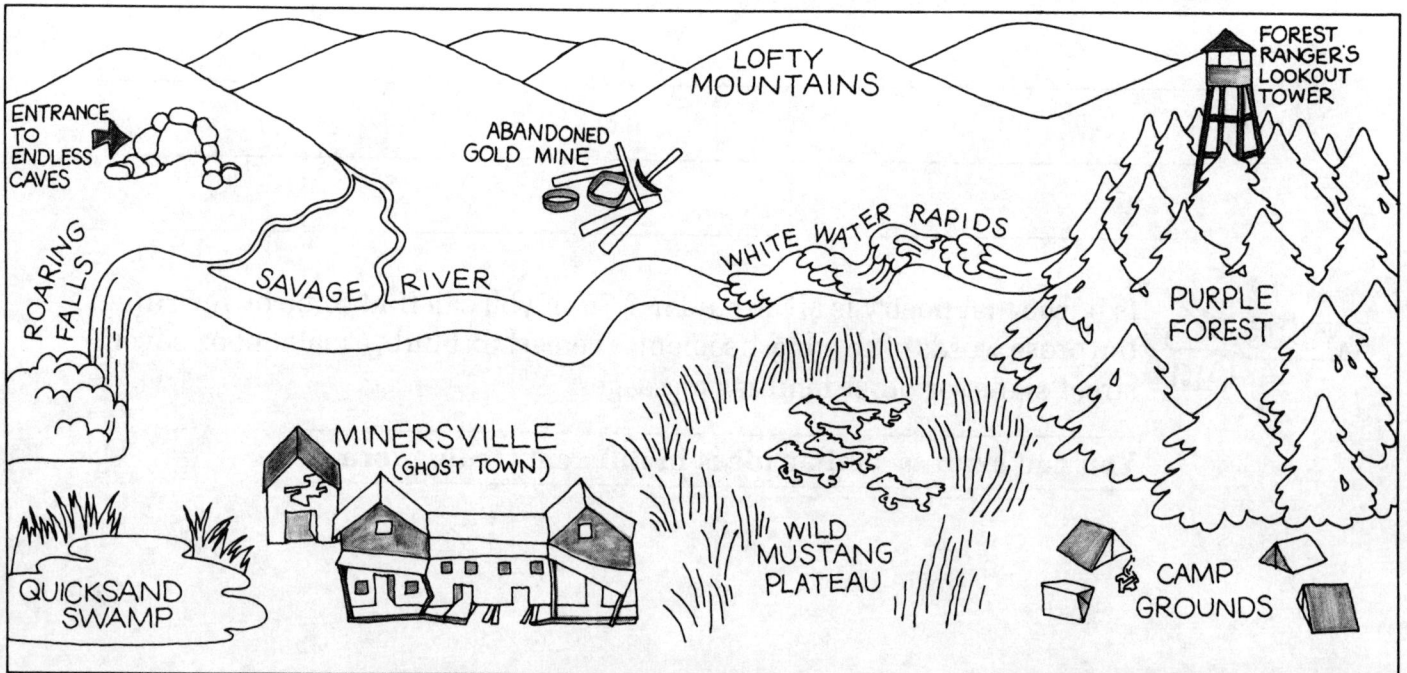

B. At the bottom of page 118 is an adventure map. Put yourself in it. Write a fictional first-person narrative telling what happened as you explored this territory alone.

_____

_____

_____

_____

_____

_____

_____

_____

In the first-person narratives you wrote for parts **A** and **B,** you were writing about yourself. But in stories, the first-person narrator is usually a character created by the author. The author puts herself or himself "inside" the character, telling how she or he thinks, feels, and experiences life.

Write On   Choose a well-known fairy tale or fable character, such as Cinderella or the boy who cried wolf. Become that person. On another paper, retell the story about that character, using a first-person narrative.

A first-person narrative is a straightforward telling of events using the pronouns I, me, my, and so on. Story writers using the first person often put themselves "inside" a character they have created.

---

4 Writing a third-person narrative

In a **third-person narrative,** the writer is not part of the story and does not pretend to be. No first-person pronouns are used, except in direct quotations. The writer can include different viewpoints and often seems to know everything about the characters, setting, and plot.

Look at the difference in these two passages.

First Person: My knees grew weak. "Who are you?" I asked, my voice quavering.

Third Person: The explorer felt his knees grow weak. "Who are you?" he asked, his voice quavering.

A. In part **A** of Lesson 3, you narrated a few minutes from your own life. On the lines below, rewrite that narrative in the third person. Do not change the basic facts. Will you change any of the events or feelings you expressed now that you can include other viewpoints?

_____

_____

_____

_____

_____

_____

_____

_____

_____

_____

B. In part **B** of Lesson 3, you wrote a fictional first-person story about your adventures in a colorful setting. Now use the setting, but take yourself out of it. Choose two or three other characters; the pictures on this page are character suggestions. Write a third-person narrative on the lines below.

_____

_____

_____

_____

_____

_____

_____

_____

_____

Write about a short incident with two characters. Write three versions. First, write a third-person narrative. Then write two first-person narratives—one from each character's point of view. Choose one of the incidents below or make up your own.

a traffic accident   a visit to the dentist
buying shoes   a first date

In a third-person narrative, the writer is not in the story and does not pretend to be. Rather, the writer can include different viewpoints and often seems to know everything about the characters, setting, and plot.

Revising and Proofreading

Polishing your writing

Do good writers always get it right the first time? Usually not. Prize-winning novelists have been known to toss away complete books and to start again. Most serious writers do two or three or four—or more—drafts before they're satisfied with their work. Few of their pages escape changes and self-corrections.

A. Reread some of the guidelines for revising given in this book. Then improve the passage that follows each guideline.

   1. Keep your nouns exact and your pronouns clear.

      The guy leading the orchestra, the one waving that thing—that stick—stamped his foot and pointed it at the guy playing the violin.

_____

_____

   2. Use strong verbs and adverbs. But don't use adverbs to make up for weak verbs.

      Olivia ran speedily to her brother's aid. She took the savage dog's tail. It went away.

_____

_____

   3. Use modifiers carefully, and keep them in place.

      Thick with weeds, Chico grew angry about the lawn; the old, smoky, balky, broken-down mower; and the price he had asked for the job.

_____

_____

   4. Some sentences need combining. But don't put too much into one sentence. Stay alert to the accents and rhythms of what you write.

Sue was cold. She was hungry. She was tired. She was lost. She had been walking through the woods. It started to rain. She had a map. It was tattered. It was old. Jim had given her the map two weeks ago. The map was out of date. It was just about completely useless.

_____

_____

_____

_____

5. Check for agreement of subjects and verbs and of nouns and pronouns.

   None of us were thinking about their job.

_____

6. Check punctuation, capitalization, and word usage.

   Abe is an all-round athlete hes good at baseball and basketball. He also run and swim good, dont he.

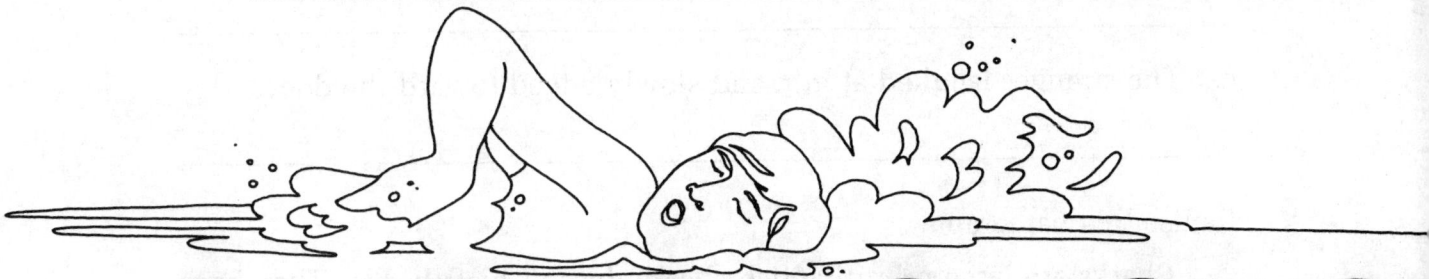

_____

_____

Look over all the "Write On" papers you have written for this course. Choose the one that you think is the best you've done. Revise and improve it on another sheet of paper.

Revise your writing until it says exactly what you want it to say and is free of grammatical and mechanical errors.

123

1. Imagine that a hurricane recently hit a beach town. Name four different writing forms that can be used to describe the event.

   _____   _____

   _____   _____

2. Below is part of a poem by William Blake. Read it and then write a short essay about the ideas expressed in the poem.

   > I was angry with my friend:
   > I told my wrath, my wrath did end.
   > I was angry with my foe:
   > I told it not, my wrath did grow.

3. Rewrite each sentence below in the first person. You may choose either character to be the first-person narrator.

   a. The stranger smiled at Brian charmingly.

   _____

   b. Brian suddenly knew that the stranger was the cat burglar.

   _____

   c. The stranger laughed at him and slowly edged toward the door.

   _____

4. Revise this paragraph.

   Sharks are large primitive fish sharks doesn't have bones. They have cartilage. Cartilage is lighter than bone. A sharks sharp teeth and powerful jaws are feared very much. Reeching a length of 20 feet, people fear the white shark most.

Answer Key

Unit 1

Lesson 1 (pages 2–3)

A. 2

B. You should have written three of these details: MacDonald left $500,000 to four cats; also left coin collection worth $10,000; 12-room house to become home for lost cats; will stated it was a token of gratitude for pets' friendship.

C. Topic sentence: Neighbors describe MacDonald as an odd, shy man.

Lesson 2 (pages 4–5)

A. 1. It's obvious from last Friday's performance that the Purple Knights need more practice to be a winning team.
2. The modern city is hard on the ears.

B. ▱ Whenever you see this symbol, check with your teacher.

C. ▱

Lesson 3 (pages 6–7)

A. You should have underlined the sentences listed under each headline.
CHERRY TREES BLOOM EARLY
The group includes Tara Tiddle, guitar and vocals; Fred Frett, bass and vocals; and Archie Armwagg, drums. They will sing "Numb Noise," "I Love Miss Mess," and other songs that they made famous with their recordings.
FAMOUS SINGERS VISIT CITY
"Oohs" and "Ahs" are heard each day from nature lovers who visit the park. This year's mild winter and heavy spring rains have caused the early blooms, according to Park Superintendent Ruth Rooty.

B. You should have underlined: *You need a map to find your way around Arnold's room.* You should have crossed out: *Arnold has a great game called "Stop the Spy." Arnold sure has a neat-looking green jacket.*

C. ▱

Lesson 4 (pages 8–9)

A. 1. My favorite time of day is early morning.
2. the second
3. You should have chosen two of these details: quiet time to plan day; can think about anything; air seems fresher; can watch new sunlight in sky.

B. ▱ **C.** ▱ **D.** ▱

Lesson 5 (pages 10–11)

A. 1. Does black cloth absorb more light than white cloth?

2. 2 ice cubes, one wrapped in white cloth and one in black, placed in sunlight. 10 minutes later, one in black cloth all melted, one in white cloth partly melted.
3. Ice cube in black warmer since black absorbed more sunlight. Black or dark clothing is warmer than lighter clothing.

B. ▱

Lesson 6 (pages 12–13)

A. ▱ **B.** ▱

C. You should have replaced each pronoun with a noun phrase like that in parentheses.
1. he (Lord Chalmers, the butler)
2. She (Suzette, Great-aunt Clementine)
3. It (the wig, the roof)

Lesson 7 (pages 14–15)

A. Suppose we never used punctuation marks or capital letters in writing. Do you think sentences and paragraphs would be hard to read? Can you see why punctuation and capitalization are helpful to readers?

B. The people had been on the island for weeks since the shipwreck. Suddenly they saw a plane flying overhead. They waved and shouted, but the plane kept going.

C. ▱

Unit 2

Lesson 1 (pages 18–19)

A. 2, 4, 1, 5, 3, 6 **B.** ▱

Lesson 2 (pages 20–21)

A. Wording may vary, but these are the ideas:
First, the thief got inside a suit of armor. Then, he moved near to the diamond and took it. Finally, he moved away with the diamond.

B. First the rooster outside crows and wakes the cat, who jumps up. Next, the string on the cat's tail moves and pulls over the water pail above the sleeping man's head. Finally, the water pours onto the man and wakes him up.

Lesson 3 (pages 22–23)

A. 5, 3, 1, 2, 4, 7, 6

B. Drive south on Court Street to stoplight. Then turn left on Main Street past First National Bank on corner. Go two blocks on Main to second stoplight. Turn left on Liberty Street past City Hall. Go past one stoplight at Broad Street. My house is the middle house on the right.

Lesson 4 (pages 24–25)

A. I. Childhood
A. Born July 4, 1940
B. Parents were song-and-dance team
C. Took dancing lessons at age 3
II. Education
A. Composed fifth-grade class song
B. Star of senior class play

125

III. Movie Career
   A. Discovered in soda shop
   B. First movie role in "Blow-out"
   C. Played lead in "The Crabapple"

B. ⇨

C. Your subheads should be under these headings:

Government	**Geography**
A. County councils	A. Coastline
B. Congress	B. Great Plains
C. King and Queen	C. Calabash Mountain
D. Royal advisors	D. Kokola Jungle

Major Cities	**Economy**
A. Grunt (county seat)	A. Zinc mining
B. Winkle (county seat)	B. Growing radishes
C. Blithney (capital)	C. Umbrella manufacturing
D. Cheeseburg	D. Leading vacation land

Lesson 5 (pages 26–27)

A. 1. No, it discusses the last heading first and the others in reverse order.
   2. B   3. the third sentence

B. ⇨

C. You might add *before, next, then, while,* etc.

D. Did you check the second sentence?

Lesson 6 (pages 28–29)

A. ⇨

B. 1. Jake baked the cake.
   2. The queen issued a decree.
   3. Two cats chased our dog.
   4. We (I) saw a speeding car on the road.

C. 1. gobbled   3. rushed, sped
   2. OK   4. lugged, hauled

Lesson 7 (pages 30–31)

A. 1. Doctor Althea J. Gonzalez, Lassie
   2. Rocky Mountains, Missouri River
   3. Minneapolis, North America
   4. Golden Gate Park, Elsie's Knitting Boutique
   5. Sunday, Fourth of July

B. 1. On, August, I, Grand Canyon, Lake Tahoe
   2. My, President Carter
   3. Last November, P. J. Reynolds, Paris, France
   4. On, Lumper's, I
   5. My, Smithville Corporation, North America
   6. Sammy's Pizza Parlor, Sunnyside Boulevard
   7. My, Stephanie, Harvard University
   8. My, Rover, Uncle Al, Christmas
   9. When I, February, Dr. Small, Liver's, I
   10. Terry Bradshaw, Pittsburgh Steelers, Super Bowl

Unit 3

Lesson 1 (pages 34–35)

A. 1. Both have a lot of stories.
   2. One sells watches; the other watches cells.
   3. Both need a batter.
   4. One holds you up; the other holds you down.
   5. When they are both mints.

B. ⇨

C. Similarities
Both are made of metal; they have similar heads, antennae, bodies, arms, legs.
Differences

1. eyes are wide open	1. one eye is half closed
2. holding gun	2. holding a bunch of flowers
3. one antenna is bent	3. antennae are straight
4. number is U2UU	4. number is B 432
5. patch on right knee	5. bandage on left foot

Lesson 2 (pages 36–37)

A. ⇨   **B.** ⇨

Lesson 3 (pages 38–39)

A. the world and an oyster
life and a web of yarn

B. ⇨   **C.** ⇨

Lesson 4 (pages 40–41)

A. ⇨   **B.** ⇨   **C.** ⇨

Lesson 5 (pages 42–43)

A. Both pictures show a young man and woman about to go for a drive. In both pictures the man is in the car, the woman is not. They are both in front of a house. In both cases the man is the driver. The girl's arms are behind her back in both pictures.

B. ⇨

Lesson 6 (pages 44–45)

A. ⇨   **B.** ⇨

Lesson 7 (pages 46–47)

A. 1. April 5, 1992, Nome, Alaska
   2. Bernier, the . . . ship, cautious, prudent
   3. Yes,
   4. surprised, Emily?
   5. pilot, the navigator, and
   6. Mars, we
   7. far-off, strange, and unfriendly, but

B. My brother loves to play practical jokes. On April 1, 1979, he carried around a water pistol, a rubber snake, and a pen filled with disappearing ink. Did he cause problems? Well, he had his fun that day, but he spent a lot of time with Mrs. Shellabarger, the principal.

Unit 4

Lesson 1 (pages 50–51)

A. You may have said: Some children are feeding ducks in the park.

B. 1. children   3. food
   2. ducks   4. trees and park setting

C. Do you notice the litter, wrongly parked van, overturned picnic bench, garbage can on tree branch, fire burning in barbecue?

D. ⇨

Lesson 2 (pages 52–53)

A. ☞   B. ☞   C. ☞

Lesson 3 (pages 54–55)

A. Answers should be similar to these:
  How it looks: yellow or white kernels covered with green husks
  How it feels: each ear is bumpy, each kernel is smooth
  How it tastes: sweet, mealy, juicy
  How it smells: sweet
  How it sounds: squeaky, crunchy
B. ☞

Lesson 4 (pages 56–57)

A. Person 1—male, bandaid on forehead over left eye, plaid shirt, right sleeve rolled up, hole in the knee of his pants, wearing sneakers.
  Person 2—female, wearing a necklace with initial "R" on a pendant, wearing dress with rip in hem, knee socks, carrying bag with comic books in it.
B. ☞

Lesson 5 (pages 58–59)

A. Janet was upset.
  She spoke in a low voice.
  A cold draft came through the doorway.
B. ☞   C. ☞   D. ☞

Lesson 6 (pages 60–61)

A. ☞   B. ☞
C. Answers should be similar to these:
  1. Ingrid glared at Jim.
  2. The train sped into the tunnel
  3. Jiro trudged across the field.
  4. Rosemaria smiled.
  5. "Hello," whispered Juan.

Lesson 7 (pages 62–63)

A. 1. was   5. are
  2. stands   6. seems
  3. are   7. wonder, are
  4. sit   8. makes
B. 1. it rains
  2. we play cards
  3. Lori bakes brownies
  4. Mark and Reginald make a salad
  5. everyone enjoys lunch
C. The cowhand walks slowly down the dusty street. He goes past the Lone Star Cafe, Rand's Hotel, and the First National Bank. Nobody seems to be around. Suddenly two shots ring out.

Unit 5

Lesson 1 (pages 66–67)

A. ☞
B. 1. I   5. O   8. F
  2. F   6. O   9. I
  3. O   7. F   10. F
  4. F
C. ☞

Lesson 2 (pages 68–69)

A. Which teams played?
  Where and when did they play?
  What was the final score?
  What contributed to one team's winning?
B. ☞   C. ☞

Lesson 3 (pages 70–71)

A. ☞
B. Did you star Favorite Subject, Favorite Hobby, and Favorite Movie, Book, or TV Show?
C. ☞   D. ☞

Lesson 4 (pages 72–73)

A. No facts. You might like to know what it is, what it does, what it's made of, how much it costs.
B. ☞   C. ☞

Lesson 5 (pages 74–75)

A. 1. The sky is yellow.   B. ☞   C. ☞
  2. ☞

Lesson 6 (pages 76–77)

A. 1. We can play tennis or chess.
  2. The day is sunny and cool.
  3. Let's go outside and enjoy the fine weather.
  4. Tony and Bertha like to play tennis.
  5. Tony doesn't play well, but Bertha does.
  6. There are courts at the high school and in the park.
B. 1. The girl on the helicopter works with the reporter.
  2. The reporter, a hero, saves the helicopter.
  3. Their boss, the editor of the paper, wants a story.
  4. The big city is filled with villains.
  5. The home under a railroad station belongs to one villain.

Lesson 7 (pages 78–79)

A. 1. referred   6. undertook
  2. overcame   7. notified
  3. sought   8. put
  4. paid   9. rebuilt
  5. wrote   10. spread
B. 1. stolen   6. bought
  2. gotten   7. knew
  3. seen   8. done
  4. heard   9. taken
  5. cost   10. wrote

Unit 6

Lesson 1 (pages 82–83)

A. A dog broke his leash and chased a cat, causing the owner to fall down. Because the dog bumped into his ladder, the painter fell into a puddle, splashing a woman and causing her to put up her umbrella. At the same time, the can of paint spilled, hitting a man and making him drop his suitcase. When the suitcase hit a man juggling eggs, he lost control of one egg, which is about to hit a woman.
B. ☞   C. ☞

Lesson 2 (pages 84–85)

A.   **B.**

Lesson 3 (pages 86–87)

A. People began building and buying houses in the desert. The new residents used a lot of water for washing, cleaning, and growing plants. But since a desert has little water, the water supply began to run low, and the residents protested to the government for more water.

B. Possible solutions: More water can be brought in through irrigation, residents can ration their water use, people can move to an area with more water.

C.

Lesson 4 (pages 88–89)

A. Cora Calmer's letter states facts and suggests a solution.

B.

Lesson 5 (pages 90–91)

A. Lightning is caused by an electrical discharge in a cloud when it comes near the surface of the earth. Thunder is a noise caused by the sudden expansion of air heated by a lightning discharge.

B.

Lesson 6 (pages 92–93)

A. Answers should be similar to these:
1. When Zeus nodded his head, the whole earth shook.
2. Since other gods also lived on Olympus, Zeus was not alone.
3. While it was daylight, Apollo rode a golden chariot in the sky.
4. Although Athena was the goddess of wisdom, she was also warlike.
5. Because Athena was patron of Athens, the city was named for her.

B. Answers should be similar to these:
1. Hermes, who was the messenger of the gods, lived on Olympus.
2. He wore winged sandals, which carried him over land and sea.
3. Hermes ran on the sunbeams which sloped down to earth.
4. Since mortal eyes were too weak to see him, Hermes came in dreams.
5. There are many Greek myths which tell about the gods.
6. We can still enjoy the myths because they are good stories.

Lesson 7 (pages 94–95)

A.
1. "How does your leg feel now that the cast is off?" Doctor Mehdi asked.
2. Tillie replied, "Much better now, Doctor."
3. "You'll need the crutches for only another week or two," the doctor added.
4. "But will I be able to tap dance?" Tillie asked eagerly.

5. "Yes, of course," smiled Doctor Mehdi.
6. "How wonderful! I never could before I broke my leg," beamed Tillie.

B.

Unit 7

Lesson 1 (pages 98–99)

A.
1. You should have put an X in the second box.
2. It bases opinions on facts. It tells what nutritionists think, what prepared foods contain, and which foods are more healthful.

B.
1. Uniform 1: It is military in style. The hat has a big visor, plume, and chin strap. The uniform has epaulets, braid, buttons, and a big B on the front of the jacket.
Uniform 2: It is a blazer and slacks costume with no hat. A white shirt or blouse with a bow tie is also worn. The blazer has a small B crest on the breast pocket.

2.

Lesson 2 (pages 100–101)

A.
1. No, they are not interested in a scientific talk. His topic isn't appropriate for an audience of dog lovers.
2. You should have checked: *How Dogs Are Our Best Friends* and *How to Teach an Old Dog New Tricks*.

B. You should have checked: *Zoo Animals*, *Why Snow Falls*, and *Kite Flying*.

C. You should have circled: *species, exemption, aeronautical, extraordinary,* and *meteorology*.

D.

Lesson 3 (pages 102–103)

A.
1. new, exciting, fun
2. It says a famous sports player has one.
3. It tells you everyone is buying one.
4. No.

B.   **C.**   **D.**

Lesson 4 (pages 104–105)

A. You might have listed titles similar to these:
More Police Needed
Let's End Parking Problems on Main Street
What We Can Do to Get Rid of Our Trash
Posters on Streetlights Must Go

B.   **C.**

Lesson 5 (pages 106–107)

A. The two puns play with:
1. *flour* meaning "ground meal used in baking" and *flower* meaning "the part of a plant that blooms."
2. *ground* meaning "broken into small bits by pounding" and *ground* meaning "earth or soil."

B.

C. You might have said:
1. Wouldn't you rather try it on in a fitting room?
2. It looks like the backstroke to me.
3. You already have one on top of your neck.

Post-Test Answers; pg 16

1. c.
2. a.
3. Answers will vary. The topic sentence should state the main idea—that a frozen lake was the scene of many activities.
4. Students' paragraphs will vary. Each paragraph should state the topic: the student's worst habit. Supporting details should explain what makes the habit lovable.

Post-Test Answers; pg 32

1. I. Aztec Culture: A and B are Arts and Religious Beliefs (in any order).
   II. Aztec Government: A and B are Three Ruling Classes and Wars with Neighboring Tribes.
2. 3, 2, 1, 5, 4
3. Paragraphs will vary. Look for correct sequence and use of sequence words. Also be sure that the topic is stated clearly and developed by each sentence.
4. Possible answers:
   a. Bert snapped a picture of the UFO.
   b. The ocean waves glistened in the sun.
   c. The magician amazed the audience.

Post-Test Answers; pg 48

1. Paragraphs will vary. Be sure students contrast the age, clothing, and other characteristics of the two people. They should also mention what each is holding.
2. Answers will vary. Possible answers are:
   (similarities) the cloud and boat both float and they can travel in any direction;
   (differences) a boat can be steered and a boat can also sink.
3. Answers will vary. Possible answers are:
   (metaphor) The math problem was a patch of quicksand.
   (simile) My younger brother is as jumpy as a kangaroo.
4. a. Laurel was born on May 23, 1971.
   b. We ordered a sandwich, a bowl of chili, and two glasses of milk.
   c. No, I haven't seen *Star Troubles*, but I may see it next Saturday.

Post-Test Answers; pg 64

1. The following details should be crossed out: *Owns a pet cat and dog* and *He reads three newspapers a day and does the crossword puzzles.*
2. Possible answers: velvety petals; sharp thorns; fragrant flower; white, pink, or red petals; green stem.
3. Paragraphs will vary. Look for a detailed description of the "suspicious," including size, coloring, distinguishing features, clothing, expression, gestures.
4. Possible answers:
   a. Erica *urged* the school to build a new gym.
   b. The accident *shocked* us.
   c. Kristen *scurried* away from the angry bull.

Post-Test Answers; pg 80

1. The paragraph is part of a feature story because it includes some of the writer's opinions.
2. Testimonial b is more convincing because it uses facts.
3. Paragraphs will vary. Anecdotes are true stories. They should illuminate some aspect of the subject's character by showing how she or he acted during a specific event.
4. a. Jon and Frank, who are identical twins, play practical jokes.
   b. Isis, a Siamese cat, won first prize at the Chicago Cat Show.
   c. The new car had a tape deck and stereo speakers.

Post-Test Answers; pg 96

1. a. It explains how the earth was made.
   b. A possible answer is that P'an Ku's voice became thunder.
2. a. Resolution: The American colonies broke away from England (or similar answer).
   b. Resolution: (Answers may vary.) People used less fuel.
3. Paragraphs will vary, but they should state four effects. You may wish to have students underline any cause and effect words they used.
4. a. The map, which was very old, led us to the treasure.
   b. Tammy couldn't play softball because she broke her leg.
   c. Nina, who was born in Ecuador, speaks Spanish and English.

Post-Test Answers; pg 112

1. *Rose-sweet, springtime scent,* and *fresh, clean flavor* should be underlined.
2. b
3. b and c
4. Paragraphs will vary. Look for opinions that are based on facts. Be sure that each sentence relates to the topic of parachuting lessons.
5. Answers may vary slightly.
   a. Martha fed the ducks which were quacking shrilly.
   b. After Stan tossed and turned all night, his eyes looked tired.
   c. Racing for the school bus, I dropped my books and papers.

Post-Test Answers; pg 124

1. Possible answers include: poem, news story, essay, short story.
2. Essays will vary. They may either restate the poem or describe thoughts that were suggested by the poem. Be sure students have understood the two points made by the poet: Anger ends when you discuss it with a friend. Anger increases when you don't confront your enemy.
3. Answers will vary. Possible answers:
   a. The stranger smiled at me charmingly.
   b. I suddenly knew that he was the cat burglar.
   c. The man laughed at me and slowly edged toward the door.
4. (Answers will vary slightly.)
   Sharks are large, primitive fish. Sharks don't have bones. They have cartilage, which is lighter than bone. A shark's sharp teeth and powerful jaws terrify humans. People are most afraid of the white shark, which reaches a length of twenty feet.